AARON'S ENER

An Unexpected Journey Through Gri
With My Brilliant Son

Second Edition

Published by Camille Dan April 14, 2021

www.aaronsenergy.com

Cover Art by Jonathan Dan

Contents

1

Aaron's Energy

An Unexpected Journey Through Grief and the Afterlife with My Brilliant Son

Second Edition

Preface

Knowing that this is a true story will not make it more believable. I, myself, wouldn't have believed it either. An open mind will help.

I didn't write this book on my own. I had lots of help. I have never been an author. I never even thought about writing a book, nor have I had the time. But, if I had, it certainly would not have been this one. I could never have imagined or expected any of what happened. I would rather none of it did, and that I had no reason to write about it.

I have no background, experience, or formal education on the subject matter of this book. My interests and education were primarily focussed on the sciences, particularly medical science. So, if I ever did write a book, it would have been about something "sciencey".

It all started with keeping a journal after my son, Aaron, suddenly and unexpectedly passed away. My friend strongly suggested it. She said, "Write everything down so you don't forget." I started right away. Grief was affecting my memory, so a journal was a good idea. I found it therapeutic. The distraction of writing provided me some relief too.

2

I took a course in writing about my grief. It helped me through the pain, and to be a better writer at the same time. My course submissions appear in italics throughout my journal.

After a few entries, my journal began to form a theme based on after-life messages from Aaron. Could this possibly be real? Is Aaron contacting me from across the veil? My doubting mind was telling me, no.

But Aaron kept slow dripping me with signs that I couldn't ignore until I finally woke up and let go of my skepticism. His messages were incredibly wondrous and transcendent. I began to discover a whole new world. I could no longer keep this all to myself.

In writing "Aaron's Energy", I have expanded my understanding of love and loss, and of life and death. My openness to possibilities has widened beyond what I thought were the ultimate limits of existence. Writing this book has been of immeasurable help to me. If reading it can help even one other person, I feel sure it will be the one who needs it most.

I wrote this second edition as an update on the miraculous things that I have journaled since writing the first. If you already read the first edition, you will find my updated entries and additional recommended reading at the end of this book.

My son, Aaron, passed away suddenly by tragic accident, on September 22, 2019. He was just 31. He fell. The circumstances surrounding his accident are still unclear. They've been unclear since it occurred. I'd like to think that it was an accident. But there was evidence left behind in his apartment that someone was with him at the time. The police investigation is still ongoing.

They haven't told me much, except that there was a "recent development" in September 2020. No closure. Was it an accident? Was it murder?

My grief is unfathomable. I heard on the radio in the car that a body had been found at his apartment building. Somehow, I knew it was him. I held my breath and clenched the sides of my seat so tightly that my handprints are probably permanently embedded. That moment is forever cemented in my brain. The flashbacks come with the force of a tidal wave of shock and trauma.

Aaron's qualities were numerous. He was wise well beyond his years, highly intelligent, intuitive, and insightful. He was witty, sensitive, and curious. He was also kind, generous, loving, and forgiving, with limitless warmth and consideration for others. He had a magnetism that radiated from him, and everyone around him readily felt his energy. I used to say that he had an "Old Soul". My grief from losing him is unimaginable. The pain is crushing and excruciating. At the same time, it is disorienting, confusing, and paralysing. It's at least, as deep as my love for him. I feel adrift and untethered. I'm exhausted all of the time. It's like I'm lost and irretrievable. I can't find myself and believe I might never. There are days when I feel like I can't live without him, or don't want to.

Child loss is unspeakable. I still have a hard time using the "D" word. Death. There, I said it. I never even uttered it for the first year. The closest I got to saying it was that my son had "passed away". It still doesn't sound right.

Aaron and I were so close. We spoke every day. We said, "I love you", so often without ever wearing it out. We shared our triumphs and struggles. My love for him was unlimited and unconditional. I had so much pride in my son and he deserved every ounce of it.

I'm still in shock, and traumatized. He was my eldest child, the first to make me a mom. His birth was the best day of my life. He and I shared his first three years of life exclusively before my second, third, and fourth children were born (the other three best days of my life).

The disbelief of child loss is not hard to understand. No one expects to outlive their own child. Equally as unexpected, especially for me, is all that has happened since Aaron's passing. I'm talking about the stuff that you'll probably have a hard time believing. But hopefully after you're finished reading, your mind will have opened up, even if just a little.

Losing Aaron has changed me in so many ways that I never would have expected. My heart is still broken, and forever will be. I lost a part of me. The me that I was is gone.

But my mind is open to much more now. I was never a writer, yet I began to write. I was never a poet, yet I have found poetry within myself. I wrote my first poem in the early days of my grief. I never thought myself a medium, or a channeler, either. But wait until I tell you about that. It wasn't very long after Aaron passed when he began communicating with me about energy and the universe.

Part I

Before Life

Love Stays

I held on to love for a fleeting moment

But it didn't want to be held for too long

It wanted to exist in eternity

And flow through time and space

It wanted to take shape

It wanted to grow and expand

It wanted its freedom

To leave and return

But never really leave

It wanted to be permanent

But not fixed

It wanted to share

But to also be selfish

It wanted to be broken

To show its strength

It wanted to endure

And be remembered forever

Camille Dan 2019

When I was five months pregnant with Aaron, I had an out-of-body experience. I don't know why it happened, but suddenly I found myself floating near the ceiling, looking down at my body lying on a bed. I felt like a coagulation of particles, or points of light. I could see everything in the room and could sense all the energy of the universe. I felt a pull, or attraction, toward the energy outside. I looked for easy escape routes from the room, like a screen or a vent, through which I knew I would meet less resistance than I would from a wall. Walls are less penetrable because they are more solid. I knew all about the universe, and that I could travel through it and explore it as I pleased.

I knew how everything worked. Just before leaving, I glanced back at my body to say goodbye. I noticed that I was pregnant and wondered if being outside of my body would somehow harm the baby in it. In a sudden rush, I was sucked back into my body as particles of light rushed away from me in the opposite direction. Just as suddenly, I came to. When I woke up, I remembered the experience, but I lost most of the knowledge I had while out there. I realized that I couldn't possess that knowledge, or understanding, while trapped within the limits of my own physical body.

Still, being a practicing nurse at the time, I decided that the OBE was some kind of stress-induced phenomenon. I was never a believer in the supernatural, or spiritual realms. My opinions were rooted in empirical, scientific data and observable, measurable information. I explained my OBE away to myself as a natural reaction of my brain's temporoparietal junction to the elevated stress I was under.

7

During my nursing career I saw some medically unexplainable things happen. I thought nothing more of them as acceptably enigmatic. One patient of mine went into cardiac arrest when I entered his room on night shift. I walked in as he flatlined. His eyes rolled backwards, and he slipped out of consciousness. It all happened within a second. I called a "Code Blue", and initiated CPR. Within a minute the crash team arrived, intubated him, and performed artificial respirations and chest compressions. It was touch and go for at least twenty minutes as we worked to resuscitate him. When we finally got a pulse, the team whisked him away to the ICU. He remained unconscious and in critical condition for days. A couple of weeks later, he was recovered and back in my care. When I entered his room, he had a big smile on his face and said, "Thank you for saving me, I saw what you did." How did he know that it was me there when he coded? How did he know what I did? He was unconscious for the entire event. Did he undergo an OBE? Stories like this were always interesting to me, but I was satisfied leaving them as unanswered mysteries.

I was as big a fan of horror films and scary urban legends as the next girl. But spiritual mumbo-jumbo was not my thing. Even after I learned that I had been seeing auras my whole life, I held fast to scientific fact. Anyway, I thought everyone could see what I saw, colours radiating from people and things. I found out later in life, that not everyone could.

My pregnancy with Aaron wasn't easy. I developed a slipped thoracic disc near the end of the first trimester and had to be on bed rest for three weeks. The doctor told me that I might need surgery to prevent my spine from being severed. But, the bed rest worked, and I was up and around after the three weeks on my back. Later in the pregnancy, I began to have early contractions that were too early. I was put on a medication to stop the contractions. Aaron was born on his due date, November 15, 1987, at the Jewish General Hospital in Montreal.

Part II

During Life

Enter Life

Aaron was a big baby, 8lbs. 5oz. The doctor did a mid-forceps delivery after hours of trying to get him out. The umbilical cord dropped too low, and Aaron's head was compressing it. He was going into distress, so they made the urgent decision to use the forceps. I just wanted him to be okay. His face was swollen when he made his appearance, but he was the most beautiful and perfect baby I ever saw. He got more beautiful with each day.

It seemed like the sun was shining from Aaron every time I looked at him. His eyes were bright, and his face showed that wheels inside his head were always turning. He took short sleeps, maybe so he wouldn't miss anything. He was infinitely curious, and forever full of smiles.

He loved to go out for rides in his stroller or the car. He'd fall into the deepest, most peaceful sleeps. There's something so angelic about a sleeping baby, and Aaron had that slumberous heavenly glow. One sunny January day, as I walked Aaron in his stroller, we met a new friend. Arlene was pregnant with her second child. We hit it off, and we've remained friends to this day.

As it turns out, Arlene is my friend for life and after-life. If it weren't for her, I wouldn't have written this book. Arlene has been there through it all. She has had many spiritual encounters and experiences. I'm convinced she is a natural-born medium. She delivered me Aaron's first message from across the veil, a few days after his passing.

When Aaron was still an infant, it became apparent that he was ahead of developmental expectations. He said his first words at eight months. He could speak in sentences before he was a year-and-a-half old. At 15 months, he could identify letters of the alphabet on Sesame Street. At two years old, his grandfather brought him a video game cartridge from Japan with 40 video games on it. Aaron could already play Nintendo Super Mario Brothers. The first screen of the cartridge displayed a list numbered 1 to 40 with Japanese writing beside each number. In no time, Aaron knew how to scroll through the list to the game he wanted. He knew the names of every game, and how to play them. I remind you that he was only two years old. He played video games with my friend's six and seven-year-old sons.

When Aaron was two years and ten months old, he loved to go for walks with me through the subway tunnel from our apartment building in Westmount to the nearby shopping centre. He made sure we took change with us for giving to the buskers. He liked to put the coins in their open instrument cases, or in their cups.

One day, he insisted on taking some coins to school with him. He wouldn't stop crying until I told him that he could take them if they stayed in his pocket. An hour after I dropped him off, the principal called. I was afraid to answer the phone. I thought that she was calling to tell me that some kid choked on one of Aaron's coins. But she said that she had to call to tell me that Aaron came to school with coins.

Then she said that he gave one to each student telling them to put their coins in the Tzedakah Box for charity. She said that she had never seen a child that young do something like that. I was very proud of Aaron, and at the same time, relieved.

On Aaron's third birthday, his brother Zachary was born. Aaron told everyone that he got a baby brother for his birthday. He came up with that on his own. Their relationship was precious and loving. Aaron adored his little brother, Zachary. He looked up to Aaron and wanted to do everything Aaron could do. My heart was so full.

When Aaron was four years old, we were driving on Causeway Blvd. to Lakeside Mall in New Orleans. We moved there in the summer of 1991. New Orleans was a wonderful place, full of culture, colour, entertainment, and beauty. New Orleans runs on "N'Awlins" Time. Sometimes, I had to pinch myself to remember that we didn't move back to the 1950s. We got used to being New Orleanians, and we loved it. Yes, it still has its underbelly, but as long as you mind your behaviour and your safety, it's a great place for families. As we drove on Causeway, Aaron asked me if I remembered when we were together, long ago, before the dinosaurs, and we traveled the universe from planet to planet. He said that he remembered it clearly, and it was fun. It reminded me of my out-of-body experience when I was pregnant with him. Was he with me while I was out there in space?

Aaron was a strikingly beautiful child with dreamy blue eyes, light brown hair, and a peaches-and-cream complexion. He started elementary school at Isidore Newman School in New Orleans. The school required academic testing results to be in at least the 95th percentile. Aaron tested in the 97th percentile. He did very well in school there, and he made lots of friends. His teachers loved him. Some of the kids competed to be friends with Aaron.

I had four miscarriages while we lived in New Orleans. It was a difficult time. It was discovered by a specialist that I had a disease called adenomyosis, a type of endometriosis. I was treated for it, and then got pregnant with Jonathan. I spent seven months of the pregnancy restricted to bed.

Every day, Aaron collected Zach and a pile of books to read in bed. We told stories, sang songs, and looked out the window. The boys danced for me in my room. They jumped up and down on my bed. Aaron made the whole thing fun, and the time pass quickly. I was surprised to have a healthy baby boy in the end. Aaron welcomed his new baby brother lovingly. All of the hardships of the pregnancy were quickly forgotten.

When Jonathan was only five weeks old, I got a call from an adoption agency that we had been chosen by a birth mother to adopt her baby. It slipped my mind after all the miscarriages, and Jonathan's birth, that we had been on their adoption list. I was happily busy with my two young boys and their new baby brother. But I wanted to go ahead with the adoption anyway.

Shelby was born a few months later. She was a beautiful, tiny, and delicate baby. Only 4 lbs. 5 oz. Aaron loved his new baby sister. He was helpful and careful with her. One day, I found her in her crib not breathing. She resuscitated easily but ended up in NICU on a ventilator for double pneumonia and a collapsed lung. Aaron was so concerned and understood more than I thought he would at his age. Miraculously, she recovered well and came home after a month. Aaron treated her like a China doll. But our tiny, delicate baby girl had incredible strength and willpower.

In Junior Kindergarten, Aaron's teacher asked him to teach his class about dinosaurs. She told me that Aaron knew more about dinosaurs than she did. At home, Aaron collected dinosaur action figures. He loved to play with them and set them up together in corrals.

One time, while playing "Dinosaurs" together, I put the T-Rex in one of Aaron's fenced-in scenes. He immediately pulled it out saying, "Mom, don't you know that T-Rex lived during the Cretaceous Period? This scene is the Jurassic Period." He definitely knew his dinosaur facts.

The Steven Spielberg movie, "Jurassic Park", opened when Aaron was five years old. He begged me to take him to see it. The trailers looked too scary for a five-year-old, so I told him that he was too young to go. Besides, it was rated PG-13, so I couldn't take him. "Mom, pleeeaaase! My friends get to go!" He was very persuasive in a cute, and way-too clever way. I gave in and took him to a matinee.

After the movie, we walked silently back to the car. I wasn't sure how he had been affected by seeing it, and I was a bit afraid to ask. So, I came up with, "What was your favourite part of the movie?" He neatly responded, "The herd scene. The graphics were amazing. At first, I thought they were Velociraptors because of their bird-like legs. But then, I realized they were Gallimimus." I was, of course, speechless.

Life

When Aaron was eight years old, we moved to Toronto where Aaron's father took a new job. During our time in New Orleans, I raised the kids, worked part-time in the ICU at Ochsner Hospital, and sat on the Sisterhood Committee at our synagogue. I secretly called myself, *"The Husbandless Wife"*. I made some wonderful friendships, some of whom I am still in touch with. After four wonderful years in NOLA, it was time to depart. The kids and I were so sad to leave our New Orleans life behind.

Things began to turn shortly after moving to Toronto. Aaron's paternal grandmother, Judy, passed away. Aaron was old enough to feel grief. He was heartbroken. He had a warm, loving relationship with his grandmother. She was so gentle with him. She was an artist and nature-lover, and she taught Aaron in great detail about the things she loved. I recall on one ravine walk Judy picked up a fallen maple leaf. She examined it closely with Aaron. She explained why the colour had changed from green to rust, and why the leaf had fallen. She showed him the stem and veins and explained how the tree fed the leaf. Aaron clung to her every word. Other times, she spent hours with him reading, drawing, colouring, and making up poems and songs. She was a remarkable woman who left a remarkable impression on her young grandson.

Schools were different in Toronto. Aaron wasn't challenged, and his performance in school went down. We didn't know what was wrong. Our obviously intelligent son was reported to sit in class staring out the window all day. We moved him to a private school, where things weren't much better. So began a lifetime of emotional struggles.

We couldn't understand what had happened. Aaron had been the model student. His verbal skills were far above average. He learned quickly and had a photographic memory. Now he was floundering in school. At home, he was still his brilliant self. We decided to take him for academic testing again. Someone recommended taking him to PACE, The Academy for Gifted Children. He seemed to be following the path of a gifted child. There, he tested in the 96th percentile.

I took the results back to Aaron's school principal, planning to tell her that he was leaving. We had Zachary tested, and he was leaving too. He tested in the 95th to 97th percentile. The problem seemed to be that both boys were bored.

The principal asked if they could stay at the school if their curriculums were tailored to meet their needs. We agreed to try this approach which we thought would be less disruptive for them. No one knew much about gifted children in those days, much less how to teach them. It was the early days of individualized learning.

Aaron came home with a reading assignment the next day. He was the only kid in his class who was allowed to pick which book to read. He scanned the shelves of our library and landed on, "Beowulf". He was in the fifth grade. I told him that book was too advanced. "Let me try it, Mom." He took it to his room.

A half hour later, he was still in his room. I went up to check on him, expecting to find him playing and not reading. Yet, there he was reading the book, a number of pages in. "How's the book?", I asked. "It's good, Mom". "Really? You understand it?" He answered, "It's not easy at first because of the ancient language, but after you get the hang of it, it gets easier". Later, I opened the book myself to see what he meant. On the first page it said, "Untranslated Version". Aaron was able to decipher, on his own in fifth grade, 11th century old Anglo-Saxon! His teacher said that this book was difficult university-level reading.

When Aaron was about twelve years old, we moved to Ohio. It was Aaron's Bar Mitzvah year, and another upheaval. Speaking of upheaval, by the end of the same summer, we all moved back to Toronto again. Aaron's Bar Mitzvah service was in Ohio, and his party was in Toronto. He seemed to handle the frequent relocation well, but under the surface he was definitely not okay.

Aaron was deeply affected by the divorce between his father and me. It was evident. He was sixteen. By the time Aaron was eighteen, at the age of his own consent, he refused to see a counselor. He was given his own apartment, credit card, debit card, and sports car. Aaron drifted into an unhealthy lifestyle and social group. He began to experiment with drugs.

Aaron was cut off from what he had been given due to the drug use. He came to me in desperation. He agreed to get off drugs if I let him move back in with me. This was not an easy contract to uphold for either of us. But, after some difficult adjustments, Aaron was on the road to recovery, health, and stability. I was proud of him.

At the same time, I feared the slippery slope of rehab. Underneath my mask of strength and helpful determination, I was scared for Aaron. Fentanyl had recently reared its lethal head on the streets. There were daily news reports of hundreds of Fentanyl-related ODs and deaths. Aaron knew about the dangers and told me he would never go near it.

Truth is, no one chooses addiction. I wish people would stop stigmatizing addiction by calling it "abuse", as if it's a choice. I think more people would seek help. Problem is, they don't go for help in part due to the stigma. Many people begin their road to addiction with prescription medication. They need medical help to get off it. But that help is inadequate.

Illicit drug pushers make it easy to get deeper into dependency. Now, criminal manufacturers are disguising Fentanyl as other, less harmful drugs. Or they're hiding it by mixing it in with less harmful stuff. The death toll is staggering. Hence, my fears.

During the time he lived with me, Aaron became himself again. He was a pleasure to be with. His bright smile was back. His energy was good. He worked very hard, and he accomplished a lot. It was incredibly hard work to come as far as he did while going through rehab. He completed his degree in Business Management and Administration and worked as an Investment Analyst. He moved into his own apartment and blossomed into the wonderful person that he was. But, for years he lamented over his broken relationship with his father.

I don't think that there are many people who can come as far as he did under those circumstances. It takes superhuman strength. Aaron retained his kind, considerate, empathetic nature through it all. He was a loving and caring son, brother, and uncle. He was also a loving, caring owner of his 110 lb. Rottweiler/Shepherd mix, Muffin. She was his devoted companion. She didn't know her own size or strength. She thought she was a lap dog. If only you could have seen the love for Aaron she had in her eyes whenever he walked in the room.

By the time Aaron was 28 to 30 years old, he was more settled with himself, more mature. He found a relationship with his father that worked for him and began to let go of the one he wished they had. He was beginning to forgive his father and to express empathy for him.

17

Aaron was spiritual his whole life. He believed in HaShem, the Hebrew name for our Lord, and he studied Judaism, mostly on his own time. He devoured books on religion and history. One Shabbat evening, we were invited to our rabbi's house for dinner. The rabbi opened a discussion about the week's Torah portion, the section of the Pentateuch read in the synagogue on Saturdays. Aaron stunned the rabbi with his depth of religious knowledge.

Aaron referred to the Torah often and was able to cite many examples from it. Because of his highly analytical mind, he could offer enlightening interpretations of the stories. His verbal intelligence was remarkable. He could make difficult concepts easy to understand. He was the only one of my children who eagerly attended services with me at our synagogue. He always led our holiday dinners and understood the blessings. I think his spirituality helped him heal quite a bit.

A couple of days before his accident, Aaron and I had dinner together at our favourite pizza place. We laughed and joked as usual, and we talked about his plans for the future. He was planning to buy and renovate a town house, or semi-detached. He wanted advice about the best way to finance it. He had already spoken to a real estate agent and scheduled a tour of available homes on the market. This was a serious, well-thought-out plan. Three days later he was gone. How could this happen?????

Part III

Journal of Grief and the After Life

Monday September 23, 2019.

My doctor put me on sedatives when I told her that I was in a state of shock after losing my son. Breathing hurt. My chest was crushing. I couldn't take a deep breath. It felt like I was having a heart attack. When the police came to deliver the terrible news, I just sat there speechless. I could barely move. I just stared into space. I might have nodded my head a couple of times.

Wednesday September 25, 2019.

I barely remember sitting in the office at the funeral home. I agreed to whatever the staff there told me needed to be done. No one expects to be preparing a funeral for their child. It was surreal. But my shattered heart still knew what Aaron would have wanted. Even in that state of shock, disbelief, and fog, I set out to honour him and his wishes.

Thursday September 26, 2019.

I don't remember much of Aaron's Shiva, but I do remember insisting that Aaron would have wanted everything traditional. Anthony covered all the mirrors. My rabbi, and some relatives put together a minyan for prayers each day. Ten men gathered at my house to pray for Aaron's transition to the afterlife, and to comfort me that his soul will get there. I remember my dear friend, Cindy, looking after things and helping make sure everything was done right. All of this went on around me, while I sat catatonic in a chair.

People and food were coming and going. Most people came over to me to express their sympathies and condolences. There were a few who said surprisingly hurtful things, meaning well, but not knowing what to say. A couple of people had the chutzpah to ask me how it happened. I guess their curiosity got the better of them. I responded calmly, "It doesn't matter how it happened. It matters that it happened."

I remember the disbelief, feeling like I shouldn't be at my son's Shiva. It was like being in a horrible nightmare that wasn't going away. I just wanted my son back. Where was he, and when was he coming through the door?

When the Shiva was over, Cindy told me she felt and heard Aaron there. I thought she said this to comfort me. Cindy is a chaplain who specializes in pastoral care. We've been friends for over twenty years. We think we might be relatives from generations ago. Cindy's father helped us figure it out. He told me that I had a Hungarian background, and I resembled someone from his family. I didn't believe him until I looked into my mother's family ancestry. Sure enough, he was right. My mother's ancestors were originally from Hungary. Never doubt Cindy's father. I soon learned not to doubt Cindy, either.

Sunday September 29, 2019.

Arlene came over to tell me she had a psychographic experience. When she saw what she had written, she knew it was a message from Aaron. He wanted her to tell me what was in the message. She told me that he came to her

20

because I wasn't open enough to hear him due to my profound grief.

When I saw the letter, I knew for sure it was a message from Aaron. It had to be. Arlene must have channeled him. There was information in it that Arlene couldn't have known. The information was very specific so that I would know it was from him. The next day, the detective in charge of Aaron's case said something word-for-word from the letter. That was my first "wow" moment.

Arlene told me that Aaron told her that I should write down everything I hear from him. So that's what I'm doing.

Wednesday October 2, 2019.

Gary, another friend of mine, came to visit me from New York. His visit was deeply helpful. I'm not sure he realized how helpful he was. He really could have just sat there and said nothing. He lost his son two years ago. His son was only 28. Gary is two years down this road. Just sitting with someone who gets it, was a comfort. But something he said touched a nerve. It was about parental guilt. He said that it's hard to enjoy things, or laugh at something funny, without the guilt kicking in. I knew what he meant. Maybe I might not feel as guilty if I could think of things as comforting, rather than enjoyable or funny.

Thursday October 3, 2019.

Lots of people get tattoos to memorialize their loved ones. I've seen beautiful, and creative personalised body art. I'm thinking seriously about getting one. It will have Aaron's name in it. I'm not sure about the design yet, but I know the right one will come to me. I won't tell anyone before I get inked. They'll try to talk me out of it.

Somehow, within days of his passing, I had the presence of mind to put on the charm bracelet Aaron gave me. It's all that I could think of that would provide me a constant tangible connection to him. I haven't taken it off.

Until I get my tattoo, I decided to memorialize Aaron with a ring made of his birthstone, Topaz. I've seen some exquisite blue ones at my friend's jewelry shop. I asked her to design the ring. It's perfect. It is in the shape of a tear. I wear it all the time.

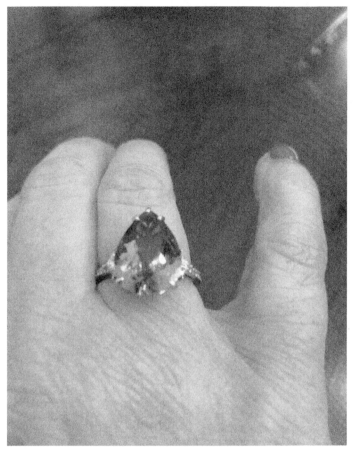

Aaron's Birthstone Ring

Friday October 4, 2019.

My friend, Cary, sent me food and a book called "Resilient Grieving" by Lucy Hone[1], a psychologist who lost her twelve-year-old daughter and two friends in a car accident. Cary has been grieving the loss of his wife for eight months. She was a beautiful person, inside and out. One of those people who radiated love and kindness. Cary is so considerate to reach out to me at this time. The book has been a real comfort. Reading it feels like you're with a friend who knows exactly what you're going through. I've been passing the recommendation forward, which makes me feel like I can help someone while I'm feeling so needy.

Saturday October 12, 2019.

I decided it was time for me to get out of town for a while. Anthony offered to take me to his cottage. It's about a three-hour drive from the city on a picturesque lake.

His cottage sits near the end of a point where the shore meets the water in a serene cove. The walk-out from the house looks onto the tops of deciduous trees and evergreens that rise from the granite escarpment of the Canadian Shield. It's a perfect place for peaceful communion with nature.

Anthony is one of those very special people who unselfishly gives of himself. He is generous with love and kindness. He's a firefighter and a great dad. I've known him for fifteen years. He's one of my closest friends. Just when we thought about becoming closer than friends, the series of

---

"Resilient Grieving: Finding Strength and Embracing Life After a Loss That Changes Everything" by Lucy Hone, Foreword by Karen Reivich, 2017, The Experiment LLC, NY, NY

traumatic losses began. I feel so blessed that he has stuck with me through it all.

By about an hour's drive out, the hustle and bustle of city life and its pressures begin to float away. I could actually put up a road sign at the site where this feeling happens. A peaceful calm drifts in. Autumn makes for a colourfully divine drive. As the front-seat passenger, I let the drone of the engine lull me into a trance as I gazed out the window.

The trees outside were beginning to change colour. The highway was lined with reds, bright yellows and oranges. I began to cry when I realized that Aaron would never see this phenomenon again. Tears were streaming down my face. All of a sudden, I heard Aaron's voice say, "I see it." Then, he said again, "I do see it Mom." I gasped. His voice was loud and clear, and very much his voice.

He went on to say that the way he sees colours now is unlike anything I can imagine. "What you see might look beautiful, Mom, but what I can see looks brilliant, vibrant, and glowing. Colours beyond explanation. I see the energy that the trees are emitting." It certainly made me feel that he was with me. He told me that he was there in the car with me, and he was also with Jonathan in his car behind me, making sure that he was driving safely.

How could this be? Was it really Aaron I heard, and not my own thoughts? His voice seemed to come from somewhere outside of my head. I could tell that it was him by the sound of his voice, the character of his speech, the tone, the words, and way he spoke. Plus, the things he said surprised me. They weren't things I had thought of.

Of course, I still doubted that it might be me hearing my own thoughts. But Aaron told me that I could hear him better as we left behind the "noise" of the city. "The less noise, the less interference, and we can connect more readily.", he said. I thought about him constantly. I was mostly depressed, sad, and exhausted. But, when I heard from Aaron, I would feel a bit better. When I felt less anxious and depressed, I would hear from him more.

At the cottage I heard from Aaron a lot. I wondered if he could see what I saw. I wondered what it was like where he is. I began to ask him questions. Many times, he would answer, "Things don't work the way you think they do, and no one alive can understand until they are where I am." He said, "Mom, I don't mind answering any of your questions that I can, but there's so much more to everything that you won't get." He told me that everything operates on a flow of energy throughout the universe.

Tuesday October 15, 2019.

On the last day at the cottage, I was feeling really low. I went to visit my friend, Karin, up at her cottage. Karin's cottage is north of Anthony's near the edge of Algonquin Park. The lake is so clear you can see to the bottom from her dock. It's a fisherman's paradise. The scenery is beyond breathtaking all year, but especially in autumn. We have shared many good times there.

Karin is one of the most productive people I've ever met. How she does all that she does with a beautiful smile while making it look easy completely escapes me. I know that it's not easy. She is unfailingly the perfect host. She's hilariously funny and highly competent. She is a true and loyal friend.

It hailed out of nowhere as I entered her cottage. It was torrential, pounding hail. Lorraine came over from her place nearby on the same lake and said that it was only hailing at Karin's. How weird. I brought my dark cloud there with me.

That evening back at Anthony's cottage, the sky was clear. As the sun began to set, from the corner of my eye, I caught a radiant glint through the picture window. I turned to look, and I saw the most brilliant rainbow arching into the lake in front of me. There was a dimmer rainbow above it. I felt Aaron's energy in the glowing rainbow. I thought that maybe my mother, who died this year in May, was in the other rainbow at Aaron's side.

Aaron's Rainbow

Wednesday October 16, 2019

Back at home in the city, I've been hearing from Aaron frequently. I can hear him better on quieter days. I ask him questions. Sometimes he tells me, "Mom, I'm busy but I'll be back." Sometimes, he answers right away. He tells me that there is no language on earth that can fully express how things work in the universe, but he tries to find the best words available to explain in ways I have the capacity to understand.

Aaron tells me that energy is always moving and present everywhere throughout the universe. "Energy is in constant flow. It's being used and emitted all the time. It can be used anywhere, for anything that happens. It has many forms that it can transfer to, or potentially transfer to. It's not necessarily specific to what it can be used for, but it does tend to go where it meets the least resistance."

He told me that energy is constantly flowing in and out of us with the universe and everything in it. He said that when a baby is born energy from the universe flows into it for use to run its body. He said, "The energy we exchange while we're alive is used for all of our purposes, physical, mental and emotional. It's important to try to keep our energy in balance with ourselves and the universe which is everyone and everything."

"Energy flows best with least resistance. But it is able to flow against resistance. We can feel when the energy we're exchanging is flowing better, or worse. When we connect with others who exchange their energy similarly to us, we make better connections, and our energy flows better. We can feel when we're connecting or not connecting with compatible energy. We shouldn't question those feelings. Questioning our feelings can create imbalance. Feelings are energy."

Friday October 18, 2019.

I try not to dwell on the circumstances surrounding Aaron's death. We may never know the whole story. I might have to accept that I'll never find out how Aaron's accident

28

happened. I already sense that it won't help me feel better to know. But I have a feeling that Aaron wasn't alone when he died. He hinted at it in the message he wrote through Arlene. I also have a feeling that one of Aaron's "friends" might know more than he's admitting. But, knowing doesn't bring Aaron back, and dwelling on this makes me feel depressed.

Aaron told me as I pondered this mystery, that friends come in all types. "There are all kinds of friends, Mom, including friends-for-a-purpose. Every kind of friend serves some kind of purpose for us, as we do for them. It's really about energy exchange and flow between people. You know by your feelings how close a friendship is, and you also know its purpose." He said that I need to get over my problem with it. He has opened my mind to learn to accept help and love however it is given.

Saturday October 19, 2019

My friend, Alison, recommended a book called "Many Lives, Many Masters" by Dr. Brian Weiss[2]. I love Alison's smarts, sharp wit, and practicality. She reminds me of my mother. She gets the job done and looks like a movie star through it. She hadn't struck me as someone interested in spiritual phenomena. We never discussed it until now.

The book is fascinating, I can't put it down. It's helping me in an unexpected way. Dr. Weiss writes about his patient's past-life regressions. I asked Aaron if reincarnation is real. He said, "People find ways to understand universal principles, and the concept of reincarnation is one of those

---

[2] "Many Lives, Many Masters: The True Story of a Psychiatrist, His Young Patient, and Past-Life Therapy" by Brian L. Weiss M.D. (Author, Narrator), 1988, Simon & Schuster, NY

ways. Since humans can't understand how energy fully works in the universe, it doesn't matter how we explain it, as long as it helps our energy flow. If it helps a person feel better to believe in reincarnation, then it's real." He added, "Energy can certainly flow from one human incarnation to another."

I asked Aaron if he believes in reincarnation. He said that incarnation and reincarnation are natural matters of energy flow that happen all the time. He said that another explanation of the same thing can be that energy is always being exchanged as it flows. "Feelings, thoughts, dreams and memories are energy that can be transferred. When a person is under hypnosis, the noise within them doesn't interfere with these energies, and they can make connections across space and time."

Sunday October 20, 2019.

Today I asked Aaron if a person can make a difference in the world. He said, "One person can cause some change in the flow of energy. Big changes in flow occur when large groups of people exchange energy similarly. Unified intent can be an example of this. Changes that are detectable on a universal scale are neither good, nor bad, they just are. The universe is consistently finding balance. We can see that in our existence with our immediate inner and outer environment. Now spread that across space and time".

My friend Arlene is interested in psychic phenomena. She told me about finding dimes. After my mother's death, Arlene paid me a visit. She sat on my sofa while we had coffee and spoke about memories of my mother.

My mother was a classy and beautiful woman. When she was young, she looked like a 1950s glamorous leading lady.

Only Audrey Hepburn did the little black dress and pearls better. She was graceful, refined, and never looked her age. She was smart too. She raised four children and ran her own business. Growing up, I was in awe of her.

When Arlene got up from the sofa, I saw a silver flash coming from where she sat. It was a dime, very visible against the dark sofa. However, neither of us noticed it before she sat down. That was quite a coincidence, eh?

Arlene and I took my dog, Maisie, for a walk in her doggie stroller. She had an operation on her knee last week. I can't walk her on her leash for eight weeks. She's getting loads of lap time. I got Maisie while on vacation in Miami last March. She was only ten weeks old. She's the cutest little mini-Maltese. I named her "The Marvellous Miss Maisie" after a favourite TV show, Maisie for short.

I was at the stage of life when my kids had all grown up and moved out of the house. I joined the "Empty Nester" club along with a lot of other baby boomers. My life went from hectic to peaceful nearly overnight. The new-found freedom that came with it felt liberating.

I could do what I wanted when I wanted. I could come and go as I pleased. I had all the time in the world to check off the things on my bucket list. I started with a two-month long vacation in Florida.

I felt wonderfully irresponsible for the first time in decades. Sure, I missed my kids when I was out of town, but I didn't miss the constant mom-life. I got too old for it. The time had arrived to be the cool, fit, jet-setting grandma. My permanent retirement had begun. At a month in, I got a puppy. Goodbye freedom. It was good while it lasted. Hello responsibility.

I have heard it said that your puppy chooses you. I discovered what that means the minute I met Maisie. Now, after all that I have heard from Aaron, I understand that it has even more meaning. She was one of a litter of four puppies, and the only one that came right up to me and snuggled into my lap. Each one was equally adorable, fluffy, and waggy-tailed. Three of them were playful with each other, but less interested in me or my lap. With Maisie, it was love at first cuddle.

At the end of our stroll with Maisie, Arlene and I stopped at her house to have a look at her newly renovated kitchen. We sat down for another cup of coffee. We spoke about Aaron and her son, Noah, when they were young. All of a sudden, Arlene spotted something in the basket under Maisie's stroller. The basket had been empty. I looked in it before the walk. But there it was, a shiny dime in the bottom of the basket. There's no way I would have missed it earlier. Since then, I've been saving every dime I've found. They seem to appear when you're thinking of someone you've lost.

Tonight, I asked Aaron about negative energy. He said, "That's something really hard to explain, but I think you're asking about bad feelings." He suggested that this is a concept beyond my understanding that wouldn't be easy for him to explain to me. "When a person is cycling energy within themselves, in the form of anxiety, anger, hate, depression, jealousy, or greed, for example, the energy of the universe just kind of bypasses it. Energy doesn't really flow well like that. But, when a person acts out on this kind of energy, it will attract with, and set up an exchange of compatible energy. When many people act out on this kind of energy, the same thing happens. The universe seeks balance. So, this kind of energy eventually ends up released to the universe to find better use. By the way, there really is no inner vs. outer environment. Everything is in constant exchange. Compatible energy is the source of creation."

Monday October 21, 2019.

Today I took Aaron's car to the dealership to return it. I was in a dense fog of grief. Anthony helped me clean out the car. We went through it entirely. It was remarkably spotless. Aaron kept things meticulously clean. When Anthony opened the trunk, there lay a lone dime glistening against the black carpet. I added it to my collection.

I've tried to take some baby steps toward an existence without Aaron physically here. It's been really tough. We were always there for each other. I hope he knows what a support he was for me. Sometimes, I felt like he was more of a support for me than I was for him. He was so wise, it was astonishing. I was often blown away by the wisdom of someone so young. I told him how wise he was. I told him every day that I loved him. Every time he said the same back to me.

Tuesday October 22, 2019.

Some baby steps forward, some backward. Last night, and the night before, there was a fly in the house. Both nights, when I sat in my chair thinking of Aaron, the fly flew directly into my face then immediately disappeared. Last night, I sat in my chair, turned on my favourite TV show, Jeopardy, and thought of Aaron. The fly flew straight at my face again, and at exactly the same time, Alex Trebek introduced the first player named Erin (which sounded like he said Aaron), and he introduced the second player from Toronto. A stunning wow!

33

Unfortunately for the fly, it was also stunned within seconds by Anthony wielding a bug zapper. My hero posed like a knight raising his sword in victory. My feelings were mixed. All I could think of, *"Was Aaron's energy in the fly you just exterminated?"*

Wednesday October 23, 2019.

When I woke up this morning, I had the fly on my mind. I felt bad. I asked Aaron if the fly should have been zapped, or not. He said that it didn't really matter. I asked him if he was in the fly. He said, "Don't worry Mom, when I need one, I'll send another." Then he said that bugs and birds are highly sensitive to energy shifts. So, they are useful as messengers, of sorts, who can look in on the living to let the departed know that we're okay. They can also be conduits that help to maintain our energy connections.

Saturday October 26, 2019.

Arlene and I were in my car in front of her house this afternoon. I was telling her about some of Aaron's communications about energy. He said that we must keep our energy flowing inward and outward in a balanced exchange with the universe. He said that when people are not physically, mentally and/or emotionally healthy, their energy cycles within them. Cycling energy this way will lead to a state that is not sustainable. While we were talking, the tree right in front of us began to glow, and the wind rustled its leaves. Just that tree, none of the others.

Aaron's Tree

Sunday October 27, 2019.

I had my first dream about Aaron last night. It woke me up.
The eerie dream began at an apartment. I was visiting a
man, about my age, who played the violin. He lived alone.
We were talking, but I can't remember what we talked
about. He had a 3X5 photograph of two children which was
scotch taped on a wall above a table. The children were on
a driveway. The boy looked about 14 years old with dyed

35

blonde hair and very dark roots. The girl was maybe 11, or 12 years old, with light-coloured hair. When I saw the photo, I turned to ask the man if he was Aaron's friend's father. He said, "Yes." After that, we walked outside and came across a young man, about 27. He walked up to the father and began to talk. The father pulled him to where I couldn't hear them. Suddenly, another young man approached. As he came closer, I saw that it was Aaron. He saw me. He was with a large German Shepherd.

He and the dog ran and jumped a fence. I chased after them, calling his name. He finally turned around. I said, "Aaron is that you?" He answered, "Yes Mom." I said, "WTF?" He said, "There were things that had to be fixed." I was startled awake.

Monday October 28, 2019.

It was very quiet when I woke up early this morning. I could feel Aaron's presence. I asked him about God and religion. He said that religion is another human attempt to understand unknown universal principles. "Energy can be exchanged through religious practice and the connections we make.

But this is very basic, and not explainable in its full scale. Like anything else, religion can help someone's energy flow with the universe. Unfortunately, conflicts over religion can arise, and cause energy to be out of flow until it returns to its best balance. God and religion are not the same thing. God is not a who, what, where, when, why, before, or after. Those are human concepts. You won't understand this until you are here."

This afternoon, Anthony and I went to Aaron's apartment to begin cleaning it. This was a painful task for me. I felt

Aaron's presence there, too. He said to me, "It's only stuff, Mom." On the way back in the car, I told Anthony how emotionally difficult it was to clean out the apartment, but I didn't feel drained because of Aaron's presence. As soon as I said that a bright orange butterfly flew in front of the windshield. I haven't seen any butterflies for at least a couple of weeks. It's late October in Canada. Yet, there was this one I saw today, so close to winter. The wow moments are mounting.

Tuesday October 29, 2019.

This morning I got up feeling guilty. Aaron said, "Don't feel guilty Mom." I asked him whose fault was his accident. He said, "There's no such thing as fault. We come across compatible and incompatible energy throughout our lives. Sometimes, it takes a long time to figure out which energy is most compatible, and which is most incompatible. When we find balance, we can feel it. Then, we can continue exchanging with energy that is balanced. When we move away from incompatible energy, it can be better used for something else."

Cary and I met for coffee this afternoon. His recommendations helped me so much in the first days after Aaron's passing. We were on the same wavelength, and he was open to reading some of this journal of Aaron's messages. We sat in a quiet corner of a small mid-town restaurant. Luckily, it wasn't busy that day. I might have been intimidated to speak about this subject in a crowded place. I think reading Cary some entries from "Aaron's Energy" might have helped him in return. It felt good to help someone. It was a good exchange of energy.

When I got home, I opened my emails. The first one I opened was from someone named Rhonda. It was sent while I was having coffee with Cary. Ronda was Cary's wife's name. Synchronicity? I think so.

Wednesday October 30, 2019.

My sister, Leah, has had many psychic experiences and contacts with loved ones who have passed. If that implies that she has lost many loved ones, she has. She has handled it all with strength and grace. Some of the most incredible signs and messages have been sent to her from across the veil.

While in San Diego visiting her family, her son went golfing with a friend of his who asked if he could invite two more friends along. When the guy introduced his friends, he said, "This is Dan, and this is Aaron." Then he said that one of them is on the Canadian golf team. Leah couldn't wait to tell me that her son felt his cousin Aaron was there.

Tonight, I asked Aaron about sin. I've been reading an intense book that an author friend of mine wrote. It's a historical account of a true story of persecution in Canada. It's very compelling and well-written. It has caused me to think. Aaron said that acting against another person, or yourself, causes energy to seek balance. He added, "Harming someone, or harming yourself makes it very hard to find compatible energy, and balance becomes difficult to achieve. The universe is pushed to move around a lot of energy. I always liked Judaism for its principle of immediate reconciliation between people. Forgiveness smoothly balances energy exchange. Atonement on Yom Kippur is an opportunity to balance one's energy with oneself and the universe. The more people work together to keep their balance, the less they have to worry about."

Sunday November 3, 2019.

Yesterday was my grandson, Caleb's 5th birthday. I felt so sad that Aaron couldn't be there for his nephew's party. He was a very gentle and loving uncle. Whenever Caleb slept over, Uncle Aaron would come to play with him, entertain him, and teach him things. Aaron had an endless amount of patience. He spoke very highly of Shelby as a mother.

Shelby is a quiet, patient mom, and an animal-lover. She's a veterinary technician and a specialist in fear-free animal care. Watching her bond with animals is none short of miraculous. She clearly communicates with them on another level. She has proven that telepathic non-verbal communication is real. Aaron admired her abilities.

Aaron and I had an enviable mother-son relationship. Aaron was so respectful, considerate, and grateful. I always told him that he would make a wife happy one day. I could tell by how well he treated me. The hopes and dreams I had for him have been lost. Our present and future were suddenly ripped away.

Jonathan told me he had a dream about Aaron the other night. He said that in his dream, Aaron's friend was repeatedly apologizing. We have all been suspicious of Aaron's friend. I think Jonathan's dream exemplified that. The guy has tried to contact us on occasion. I asked Aaron if we should respond to him. Aaron said, "It's best for all of you not to invite his energy into your lives."

I'm feeling increasingly sad. I've been crying a lot and feeling more exhausted. Maybe it's because Aaron's birthday is coming soon. Plus, people have been asking for details of Aaron's accident again this week. It sets me back to hear their questions. How can they not know how much this hurts? They don't mean to cause me pain.

I don't know how to answer them, anyway. Even if I did know the answers, I still wouldn't want to discuss it. I asked Aaron what I should do about it. He said, "You will not find the answers to all of your questions by asking about this, even when you feel that your questions have been answered."

Monday November 4, 2019.

Today we went back to Aaron's apartment to clear it out. I've been dreading this day. I had to go through his stuff and decide what to keep and what not to keep.

This task was wrought with grief. It took all of my energy to keep from falling apart. I tried to be methodical and robotic, but it's impossible not to have feelings.

I came across some of Aaron's drawings and writings. There were things there that he didn't ever tell me about. Of course, he was allowed to have his private life at his age. He was 31.

I asked Aaron if he felt okay about keeping secrets. He said that secrets can be kept for maintaining a good flow of energy. "Trust is such an important aspect of love. Mistrusting relationships are imbalanced and not sustainable. The energy will find elsewhere to go in the universal flow. In order to have trusting relationships, a person must work to find balance within themselves. No one has control of anyone else. People have the ability to control themselves. Mistrusting self, mistrusting families, mistrusting countries, and mistrusting world are all not sustainable."

Tuesday November 5, 2019.

I started reading another book a few days ago. It's called, "It's OK That You're Not OK", by Megan Devine[3]. The author, a grief counselor herself, lost her husband in a tragic drowning. This loss threw her into a state of grief she never knew, despite all of her professional experience.

Megan's account and impressions of "out-of-order" loss are enlightening, and incredibly accurate. Through her own experience, she's been able to describe the path of grieving very well. She is quite relatable.

Wednesday November 6, 2019.

Yesterday, I had to go back to Aaron's apartment for something I forgot to do. Last time I was there, I thought would be the last time I would have to go in there. All of the feelings returned as soon as I opened the door. It felt like a huge setback. For the first time, I felt anger. I was wondering if I would. Every book I've read mentions the anger associated with grief. I had never been angry with Aaron. I feel confused now, too.

Not long after anger, its partner, blame crept in. Gary told me that his bereavement group spends a lot of time on guilt and blame. These are two major concerns of bereaved parents and families. Especially for those parents who chose "Tough Love" parenting. That's when parents attempt to show their children that they will not enable any misbehaviour. Some refer to this method of parenting as "being cruel to be kind". It doesn't always work out.

---

[3] "It's OK That You're Not OK: Meeting Grief and Loss in a Culture That Doesn't Understand" by Megan Devine, Foreword by Mark Nepo, 2017, Sounds True, Boulder Colorado

There have been many studies done on this subject, and all of the research has found that there is no difference in outcomes between the two approaches. However, there is a slight increase in the incidence of early death in young people whose parents went with a "Tough-Love" approach.

I googled "Tough Love vs. Unconditional Love" and found some studies online. One study said that no matter which approach is employed by parents, the difference in outcomes depends on two factors, honesty, and love. Even if "Tough-Love" is the chosen approach, outcomes are better when the parents remind their child often that they are loved, that this approach was chosen out of love; and that it was chosen to be supportive of good choices, and not supportive of bad choices. My guess is that most parents wing it. Parenting should be part of a "Life Skills" curriculum in schools.

I sure didn't go with "Tough Love" parenting. What I did was quite the opposite. I wasn't strict enough. I might have even been one of those enablers. This is what I tell myself as I grapple with my guilt. I told Aaron I loved him every day. I involved myself. I helped my kids help themselves. Aaron sometimes told me that I was too soft. He certainly worked hard and pulled his weight. We were in this together.

After so many years of sharing rewards and progress, I was caught up in the idea that life would go from one success to the next. Now, I just feel shattered. It's easy to lay blame on yourself, and everyone else when you're so deep in grief.

I tried to connect with Aaron yesterday knowing that it always makes me feel better when we do. But the connection wasn't happening. This evening, Arlene phoned to tell me that she connected with Aaron. He told her that he wants me to use my experience to help others as a way to help myself through my grief. Aaron and I, helping others together, and at the same time, helping me. Sounds like a very good plan.

I've been telling my friend, Laura, about my experiences with Aaron. If anyone has an ounce of common sense, Laura has gallons of it. She and her family moved to New York years ago. We still visit each other often and talk on the phone in between. She reminds me of my mother. Classy, brainy, and beautiful. They often say exactly the same things. Laura has a highly intuitive, inquisitive, and logical mind.

Her friendship is grounding, so I wasn't expecting her to be too open to hear about my afterlife visits from Aaron. Yet, she was very interested. She added a logical perspective to the conversation and told me that she was learning a lot from it.

Aaron told me that he hadn't been able to connect with me because of my anger and guilt energy. The guilt feels awful. I don't know how to let go of it and forgive myself. I feel guilty for not being a good enough parent. I didn't do enough for Aaron. What if I could have done something to prevent his accident? If only I had been in the right place at the right time, he might have lived. The "what-ifs" and the "if-onlys" are eating a hole in my gut. I am the most forgiving person who can't seem to forgive myself.

Aaron had to connect with Arlene to get his message to me today. He said that he connects with me when my energy is in flow with his. He said that his energy won't connect with energy that is cycling back with itself, like that with anger, blaming, guilt, failure, self-deprecation, or self-isolation. He said that we will always easily connect whenever I'm most open with the energy of the universe.

43

Thursday November 7, 2019.

I'm having a quiet morning. The quiet gives me an opportunity to try to connect with Aaron. Consciously trying to connect inevitably forces me to acknowledge the reality of Aaron's passing.

In order to connect with him, I'm not able to live in the delusion that I'll wake up one day to find out that this was all some kind of nightmare, and life will return to normal. So, I tell myself that the connection with Aaron in this life is worth facing reality.

Aaron tells me this morning that love is the connection. "Love is energy that draws us together throughout time, and through whatever form in which we exist. We can connect with anyone and anything when we are open. In this way, we exchange energy in balance. We must be open to love. Love is balance."

I asked Aaron if there are obstacles to energy flow. Aaron said that obstacles do exist and are necessary to provide direction. "Matter is not in our way. It just helps move energy around. Matter is energy too, just flowing at different rates. Energy can enter an exchange with matter, or it can go around it. Matter slows or redirects energy toward balance. We are part of it all, Mom." He said that this is the best explanation he can communicate to me using language that I can comprehend.

Aaron says that we're lucky to have the opportunity to experience love when we're alive. Love is energy that we can understand. "Humans have the most developed ability of all earthly species because we can feel love, and we can also define it with language. So, we can feel and think love. Not all matter possesses that level of ability, and that makes us a special part of the universe. We have a unique opportunity for this form of energy exchange, and some

44

control over how we choose to exchange it. You can choose to love a purse, a pair of shoes, a car, or a rock.

Loving energy went into the creation of those things too. But, to exchange love at a higher conscious level is how life happens." Aaron recommends working to exchange the energy of love by being open to finding its fit within you.

My quiet morning was cut short by a phone call that my father fell and was on his way to the Emergency Room in an ambulance. It's the first snowfall of 2019, the traffic news sounds horrific, and now I'm about to drive an hour to the hospital on icy roads. I can feel my anxiety rising. What else can happen?? Shelby has been on crutches with a bad ankle sprain all week. I was hit in the jaw with a rocket-fired tennis ball yesterday, and I'm in pain.

Now this? Of course, none of this compares to what's already brought me to my knees. But, c'mon!

Aaron told me to stay calm, and pace myself, he and my mother are with my father and everything will be ok. He was right. I got to the hospital safely. My father's X-ray and CT scan were normal. He's already going back to the assisted-living home. Everything is ok. I'm back at home writing more in my journal.

On the way home, however, I was overcome by sadness and disbelief again. It hits hard when it hits. I used to call Aaron with updates about his grandfather, he cared for him so much. Aaron was helpful and attentive to both of my parents. He valued family. He believed strongly in the commandment to respect parents, and this showed so beautifully in how he treated his grandparents.

Aaron told me that it's ok to be sad. He insisted that he didn't mean for the accident to happen. He said, "There's no way I meant for it to happen. I'm confused about how it happened."

He said that he understands why I'm so sad. I asked him how I can avoid cycling energy of sadness. He said, "Don't worry about that, Mom, it's normal." He said that it's human to cycle that kind of energy sometimes, especially under these kinds of circumstances.

"You can't prevent having human feelings associated with loss, especially when it's so traumatic. Trying to fight them, or force yourself to feel differently than you feel, isn't balancing energy either. You must deal with your feelings honestly."

Aaron reassured me that he is always around. If my energy isn't compatible with his from time to time, it's ok. If he needs to connect with me through a friend who is open, he can always do that. There will always be times when our energies are compatible, and we will have easier, more direct connections.

Speaking of open friends, there's Catherine. She lost her mother and sister in a tragic accident. Her father passed soon after. So much horrific loss within a very short span of time. She is writing a memoir of her experience with tragedy and sudden loss[4]. We often discuss what we are each writing.

Catherine has been very supportive of me through my grief, as I have been supportive of her too. Catherine founded a charity in memory of her sister, Julie. Every year, she celebrates Julie's birthday with a fundraiser for Special Olympics. Julie was happiest in life as an athlete. At this

---

[4] "Breathe Cry Breathe: From Sorrow to Strength in the Aftermath of Sudden, Tragic Loss" by Catherine Gourdier, May 11, 2021, HarperCollinsCanada

time of year, I think a lot about Catherine. Julie's birthday was November 2nd.

I asked Aaron if Julie was there with him. Instead of hearing Aaron, I heard a young woman's voice say, "Hi Camille! I'm here, and Catherine is great. The party was great, it's always great!" She said that she's there, and her Mom and Dad are too.

Friday November 8, 2019.

Late yesterday afternoon I was visited by my rabbi and Mordechai, the executive director of our synagogue. They came to follow up on a previous conversation about establishing an initiative at the shul in Aaron's honour. Aaron really liked and respected Rabbi Elie, and he really liked our shul. Before the meeting, I thought about reading "Aaron's Energy" to them for inspiration and planning. I asked Aaron if it was ok. He said that it was up to me whether, or not, to read it to them.

After they arrived, I asked them if they would like to hear me read to them what I've written about Aaron. Before starting, I told them to stop me if they're not comfortable with what they hear. We all agreed on that.

When I got to the part about Arlene's psychographic experience, I stopped to ask them if I should keep going. Rabbi Elie said, "Please continue." So, I did. But I stopped again to check in with them when I came to the part where I heard Aaron's voice. They both said, "Keep reading." They were clearly interested.

When I finished reading, there were a couple of seconds of silence. During that pregnant pause, I thought that these guys must think that I've gone crazy. Then, Mordechai spoke. He asked me, "Have you studied Kabbalah?" I told them that I have never studied Kabbalah, but I've heard a bit about it, and Madonna. Mordechai was amazed. He said, "This is Kabbalah 101, 201, and 301!"

Rabbi Elie said, "This is the essence of Judaism." I said, "Rabbi, to be honest, I'm not a regular shul-goer." Then he said, "You wouldn't have heard of this in shul, it's very high-level, and beyond what we cover. It's about HaShem and His perfect universal plan." I told them, "I don't know where I would have learned this, then. I have to assume it's coming from Aaron."

Mordechai asked if I think that this is related to my out-of-body experience. I agreed that I saw a connection to that. I reminded him of what Aaron said when he was four years old. Mordechai said that in Judaism it is believed that an infant's soul enters its mother with all the knowledge of the universe before it takes human form. After birth, that knowledge changes into what is required for existence and learning. I didn't really see what the purpose of this process could be on a universal scale, but I did hear that it fits with what Aaron is telling me.

We moved to a discussion about what the shul could do to honour Aaron. Coincidentally, they had a plan that encompassed learning and making connections for young adults. I made sure that the program will be in Aaron's name. It will be for young people whether they are religious, or not. Everyone will be welcome and accommodated, and there will be opportunities for socializing, learning, private consultation, life skills, balancing life, and mentoring. Aaron often spoke of his concern for these matters that young adults are facing today. It sounded like a perfect way to honour Aaron, and we agreed to establish the program.

This was the first time since Aaron passed that I had a good feeling. I told Rabbi Elie that I'm afraid to have good feelings yet, so I can't say that I'm happy. He said, "Maybe you can be sad/happy about this." That sounded about right.

After they left, I realized that I was so sad/happy that I forgot to check with Aaron if he agreed to being honoured this way. So, I asked him. Before I even finished the question, I heard Aaron's voice say a very loud, "Yes!"

This is the second charity initiative I have established in honour of Aaron. I read that it's a good thing to do while grieving a profound loss, and many people do it. I feel that I can keep Aaron's interests and concerns alive and direct his energy to them. Aaron cared very much about many issues, and funds will be directed to support related causes.

I called to tell Arlene that I think the opportunity to fulfill Aaron's message of helping myself by helping others arose the day after she heard him say it. While I was telling her about it, she told me that she heard Aaron say, "I'm with you all the way Mom."

This morning I spoke to Laura, and we caught up on "Aaron's Energy". When I told her about Aaron's message to Arlene, she said that she can see how clearly therapeutic this is for me, and that it's also fulfilling Aaron's wishes. She said that I'm continuing to learn from Aaron and his wisdom, and it's helping others to learn too.

I told her that Megan Devine's book is currently helping me. It seems that reading books like this helps to augment and validate Aaron's messages. Laura said that everyone is working together, just as Aaron is saying how energy works. I responded, "I'm going with the flow."

Just as I said that I found Megan Devine's "Refuge in Grief" website and signed up[5]. Things are happening so frequently and everywhere. It's getting hard to keep up with writing them down. Aaron's energy is so powerful.

Arlene just called and told me about an experience she had last night. She has a painting in her house that she had commissioned years ago. It's of a room with a large mirror in the back. In the mirror there's a door ajar. Aaron told her to look at the painting and imagine that he is on the other side of the door. He said the universe works like that. "You are in one room. I went through a door to another. The door is always open."

In Arlene's painting, you can see the door is ajar. Look closer and you can see faces looking outward through the open door. Those faces are not in the painting, yet they are in the photo.

---

[5] "Refuge In Grief", Megan Devine, https://refugeingrief.com/

Arlene's Painting

This gave me the idea to try contacting others who have passed. After all, I've heard from Aaron and Julie. I thought about Arlene's mother. For some reason, probably my grief and age, I blanked-out on her name. Instantly, I heard a woman's voice say, "Shirley." I thought, *"Oh, right!"* Then Shirley said, "I'm proud of Arlene for being so helpful to you." The thing was, that this was definitely Shirley's voice that I heard. I recognized it right away. I had to call Arlene to tell her. She was so happy to hear this message from her mother.

Doubt set in. Of course, I doubted that I could really contact these souls out-of-the-blue. I needed proof. So, I put out this request, "If this is all real, can someone please tell me something that I couldn't possibly know, but could then be proven?" I heard Aaron say, "Mom, it's not your job to be a psychic. It's your job to help others with my message." Then Ronda's voice popped in and said, "I'll tell you something you can prove. There's a box with my jewelry under my bed."

Saturday November 9, 2019.

I'm thinking of everything all at once this morning. Yesterday, I saw Megan Devine's post on Instagram. It was about how grief changes friendships. Friends want to be helpful, but don't have the skills. They sometimes personalize your grief when trying to be supportive. It leads them to say hurtful things, even though they're trying to be helpful. This rang a bell with me, so I submitted a comment, "Signed up. Just lost my son in a tragic accident. People mean well, but it's too late after they say something stupid. The hurt button can't be un-pushed." Megan Devine posted a "Like" on my comment. When I saw her

"Like", I felt an energy connection was made. This told me I'm headed down the right road.

Arlene told me that "Aaron's Energy" makes her feel high. It's such a good feeling. I must agree with her. It's lifting me up through my grief. It's carrying me. It's pointing me in the right direction. The more energy connections I make, the better I feel. "Aaron's Energy" is helping me to grieve better.

Now I'm thinking, there must be some purpose to all of this. Is it possible for "Aaron's Energy" to help more than just me? The world is suffering an epidemic of unspoken grief.

We're living in a disconnected world. Political division is rising. Disquiet is epidemic. People are trying to come up with ways to relieve their pain, grief, depression, loneliness, and PTSD. Communities are trying. Countries are trying. Yet, we seem to be getting farther away, and deeper into suffering. This just isn't working.

"Aaron's Energy" is about connection. It's about exchange of compatible energy. What if balancing energy with each other and the universe made life better for all of us? What if "Aaron's Energy" could help to build understandings, and clear up misunderstandings? We could learn to exchange energy with ourselves, each other, and the universe and lighten each other's personal load of pain and grief. Maybe, through energy connection we can turn things around. End suffering. What if "Aaron's Energy" could do that?

Since it's necessary to be part of the flow and balance of universal energy for this to happen, we all need to learn how to connect with it. Visualization works well for me. Some people feel that meditation helps them to find tranquility within themselves. Others do deep breathing.

There are so many different methods to try. I've heard that some people find music soothing. There's also sound therapy machines and apps. The important thing is to find what works best for you to quiet your own mind.

Here's how I make my connection. I sit or lie down in a quiet place where "noise" and interference is minimal. I close my eyes and imagine a picture of what the energy around me looks like. In my mind, it looks like tiny points, or particles of light streaming around me and through me. Some are moving faster than others, some are going through me, and through all of the objects and people around me, even my dog. Animals are expert energy exchangers. Just spend some time with horses, and you'll get what I mean.

I picture in my mind some of the energy staying in me for a while, then flowing back out into the universe. Some of it is staying in the objects, the people, and the matter around. Some energy is flowing past me, bypassing me for other destinations. In this trance-like state I can see auras everywhere.

The energy that I visualize flowing into me gives me comfort. It gives me a feeling of being a bit high. It relieves my pain and grief. It motivates me to exchange this soothing energy with others, providing them with a similar feeling, that they might in turn exchange with someone else. It makes me feel like I'm connecting with compatible energy. It's in this state of balance that I'm able to connect with the energy of the universe. This is where I find Aaron.

Sunday November 10, 2019.

Yesterday, Aaron's grandfather came over to discuss "Aaron's Energy". It was an enlightening discussion. He has always had an open mind and has had many psychic experiences in his life. I have always been grateful for Leslie's concern for the kids. He takes great interest in their well-being. He's an involved grandparent. I was happy to hear that he continues to be concerned for Aaron. Aaron had a deep respect for his grandfather. Leslie had some good suggestions about how Aaron can continue to fulfill his mission through our efforts.

As soon as Leslie brought up his sister's passing, I heard her say in her voice, "I'm here, tell Leslie, Hi." Aunt Edie knew that I loved her. She was one of my favourites. I realized that Edie connected easily because the energy in the room was welcoming.

Leslie asked if Aaron has mentioned anyone else. I sensed that Aaron wasn't present once Leslie asked this question. I told him that they don't tell me much about other people, but I can ask him. I heard Aaron's answer to his question. He said, "My message is meant to be helpful to everyone."

This morning, Aaron had more to say on the subject. He said that his energy is in balance with the universe where he is now. It was out of balance in his life. That must be what he meant in my dream when he told me that things needed to be fixed. "If the energy here isn't working toward balance, I will not be the only one who will need to fix it, Mom. Everyone must work together to find balance. The best place to start is within themselves."

Monday November 11, 2019.

Today is one of my mother's birthdays. She had two birthdays: the right one, and the one that is recorded on her birth certificate. I always get them mixed up. The other one is November 14th. November 15th will be Aaron's birthday. I've been anticipating a horrible week.

Grief is incredibly powerful. I read that it's worse at birthdays and holidays. This is true, for sure. Today is also Remembrance Day. Talk about a day of powerful energy. All I can think about is how I'm going to get through this week in one piece.

I've been sending excerpts from "Aaron's Energy" out to a few friends. I've heard back positive response after positive response. Some friends even sent them to their friends and relatives. "Aaron's Energy" is spreading and beginning to have the effect Aaron intends. That's extraordinary.

Everyone's response has been unique, but there has been one similarity. People are all talking about their connections, and how their feelings have been reawakened. They are feeling their energy connections flowing and opening up to the opportunity to express them. "Aaron's Energy" is presenting this exchange of compatible energy.

One response stood out. A friend sent a recommendation to seek a prominent teacher of Kabbalah in Jerusalem. This sounded like a great idea, at first. I Googled the teacher, and he sounds incredible. He is clearly fulfilling his mission. While looking at his profile, I got a message from Aaron. The gist of the message was: don't do this now.

It made me realize that studying Kabbalah might confuse me. How will I be able to tell the difference between my own thoughts and what I'm hearing from Aaron? Never mind how confusing Kabbalah already is, it will probably confuse Aaron's message. After all, I'm getting these messages without ever spending a minute in a Kabbalah class. Maybe I'll wait for when it feels like the right time.

For now, I know virtually nothing of Kabbalah, and I'm good with that. So is Aaron.

I began thinking about all that has occurred since Aaron passed. I'm still not yet fully convinced that I'm actually hearing from Aaron, and other souls. It very well could be coming from my own mind to comfort my grief. However, the timing of these messages is significant. Why have I never come up with thoughts like this before now if I already knew this stuff? I'm keeping an open mind.

I was reminded of a message from Aaron that came as I grappled with doubt. Aaron said to keep open and keep spreading his message. He said, "It's getting crowded at the door on this side. Everyone here wants to come through and connect with everyone there."

I just got off the phone with Cindy. She told me that she's amazed by Aaron's powerful influence. She said that I'm so lucky to have continued contact with him. Not many people are so lucky. I said that I don't have any special gift, and I don't really feel lucky. I'd rather have my son here. But I understood what she meant. I believe that everyone has the ability to connect. They just have to find a way.

Cindy told me that my openness is obvious, and to keep open and keep connecting with Aaron. She said to try to remain positive. Just as she said that I heard her father say, "Tell Cindy to listen to what she just told you." He'd like to connect directly with her. When I told her what her father said, Cindy said, "You just made my day."

I spoke to my friend, Liza, today. Liza's kids and my kids grew up together. We met when our two eldest were toddlers. Memories of the kids when they were that young bring me to tears. My son should still be here too. It's so unfair.

57

Liza called responding to "Aaron's Energy" with her own stories. She told me that she has had many psychic experiences, including an out-of-body-experience that sounds similar to mine. She was aware of the energy and knowledge of the universe while out of her body, like I was. Our discussion felt like a powerful exchange of energy, which I pointed out to her. We were carrying out Aaron's message in our conversation, in real time. We agreed that everyone can find a connection to the flow of energy by being open to compatibilities.

Tuesday November 12, 2019.

Of course, the extraordinary has to be balanced with ordinary events of daily life. Thoughtful people are sending their messages of condolences for Aaron's birthday this week. If I hear the word "bittersweet", or the words "God only gives us what we can carry" one more time, I think I'll turn off my phone and never leave my house. Just to hear this stuff is so draining and takes way too much energy to correct it. My tank is too low with no reserves. It's both Aaron's birthday and my mother's birthday this week. Plus, Zach shares his birthday with Aaron. We all feel like crawling under a rock actually.

Aaron came in loud and clear this morning. I can feel that he feels my pain, and he wants to comfort me, especially this week. He told me to do what I need to do to get through. He told me not to push myself, just go with what feels comforting. "Let other's energy stay with them. Maybe they will be ready for exchange with you one day, Mom. You're not ready. Not for now."

"You know the energy you need for exchange by how you feel." Aaron said that a lot of people try too hard to say "the right" thing, do "the right" thing, or be "the right" person. They are consciously, or unconsciously, cycling their own energy trying to be perfect. "We are all really perfectly imperfect.", he said.

Aaron said that energy exchange is integral to survival. "We are all equipped with energies that help us survive. A plant, or your chair, or any other non-human matter exchange energy, but don't have choice. Animals have instincts, but not much decision-making. Human instincts of fear, self-protection, anger, comfort, and love are for survival. These energies can be in balance, or out of balance. In an example of imbalance, fear, self-protection, anger, and love can be all out of rhythm and cycling within. Both inward cycling of energy, and acting out on imbalanced energy, are ultimately not sustainable."

Aaron explained that egocentrism and narcissism are normal parts of being human and are part of our instincts that we use to survive. These instincts can become a problem when they grow beyond their level measure, just like anything else.

He's telling me about narcissism because it has grown way out of balance in our world today. "Mom, narcissistic leaders are reflections of selfish, greedy, narcissistic societies pushing things out of balance. The universe is pushing back."

"The ultimate survival instinct is to balance your energy. When people can find balance within, they will be able to create balance beyond themselves. Finding compatibility sustains energy exchange because it flows in balance. Survival depends on sustainability."

He expanded, "The evolution of humanity toward individualism will be its ultimate extinction by the forces it attracts. Human endurance extends beyond the individual. Life depends on collective interpersonal conscience. But the toxic elixir of greed, fame, identity, and selfishness has been a tempting cocktail. Without a global shift in this paradigm, the horizon on human biological existence is in sight." So, Aaron is saying that drinking the Kool Aid, another overused urban dictionary idiom, will extinguish us all. We must reunite and reignite before it's too late.

Tonight, I heard from Aaron on another subject. He told me that people have created tools of measure for use during their lives, like hours and minutes, dollars and cents, pounds, and kilograms. "People assign value to tools. Value is energy related to love. Balance or imbalance can occur depending on how the energy is exchanged. Massive individual wealth and abject poverty is an example of severe imbalance. Racism, discrimination, and partisanship are other examples. All are untenable.

Human beings are far out of balance with environmental and universal energy because of their own imbalance. They have no idea what they are up against."

There is so much imbalance in today's world. Aaron said, "It is possible for human beings to balance their energy in flow with the universe by balancing their own existence." If that can be achieved, we can all connect with each other across the veil. Aaron's message is beginning to jell.

Wednesday November 13, 2019.

I came across an interesting article about sound vibrations today. Not long ago, I wouldn't have bothered to read an article like this. But it made me think about Aaron's meaning of "noise".

In the article, Dr. Bruce Lipton, a molecular biologist, says that if he plucks on the string of one guitar, the same string on another guitar nearby that is tuned the same will vibrate[6]. Imagine all the sounds of the city going on, and all the resulting vibrations. That's a lot of noise.

Sound is energy. If guitar string G can vibrate by itself when string G of another guitar is plucked, what does that say about vibrations and compatibility? It says to me that Aaron is right. Energy travels to where it finds compatibility.

This evening, I attended a class with a friend at my synagogue taught by our Rebbetzin, the rabbi's wife. It was on modern psychology found in ancient wisdom. When the Rebbetzin spoke of Moses and the Torah, I began to drift and wonder. How was the Torah even written? Why five books?

As I sat there, I heard Aaron answer my questions. He said, "You know how you can hear me, Mom? That's how the Torah was written." He said, "The five books of the Torah represent the five dimensions that humans are capable of knowing." He said that there are the three dimensions that we can see and sense, and a fourth dimension of time relative to space. Aaron said that he exists in the fifth dimension, but his energy can cross all dimensions. He said that my energy can too, but I'm only aware of it in three.

Since I wasn't clear about what this meant, I decided to google "Torah and Five Dimensions" when I got home. I found an article called "Sanctuary in Five Dimensions" on a website called, "Quantum Torah"[7]. The article was written by Alexander Poltorak, a theoretical physicist and biomathematics professor at Cornell U and professor of

---

[6] "How to Change Our Self-Limiting Programs" by Chip Richards, November 13, 2015, upliftconnect.com, # Dr. Bruce Lipton
[7] "Sanctuary in Five Dimensions" by Alexander Poltorak, Quantum Torah, Disentangling The Bible, July 27, 2018, https://www.quantumtorah.com/sanctuary-in-five-dimensions

physics at Touro U, CUNY. He is well published in physics, kabbalah, and Jewish philosophy.

In his article, Poltorak says that in the Sefer Yetzirah, the oldest surviving book of Kabbalah, the universe is described as five dimensional. He says, "The Sefer Yetzirah's five-dimensional universe provides the answer. When God commanded 'And you shall make Me a sanctuary,' He commanded us to build Him a Sanctuary in five dimensions. The fifth dimension is the dimension of the soul. Now we understand that building the Sanctuary for God in five-dimensional universe involves building a physical Temple in space, observing the Shabbat, and building a sanctuary for God in our own soul."

The multidimensional universe is a concept familiar to both science and religion. Physicists have theorized that the universe is composed of eleven dimensions, and that Black Holes are evidence of dimensions beyond the four that are known.

Common to most religions is the dimension of the soul. Whether it be communion with God, achievement of enlightenment, entry to paradise, transcendence to heaven, or any other transition from the body to the spirit, theologies suggest that crossing to another dimension is involved. It sounds like science and religion share this common intersection of thought.

I'm speechless. Another wow! I am not a physicist, or a philosopher, or a scholar, or a Kabbalist, or anything even close.

I've never heard of Professor Poltorak. I can't pretend to be, or even be in the room with minds like this. I'm Aaron's mother. My doubts that he is communicating with me have disappeared. I'm going to keep going with the flow.

Thursday November 14, 2019.

Today is my mother's other birthday. Tomorrow is Aaron's birthday. There are no words to describe the depth of my sadness. Tomorrow, I have nothing planned. The only entry in my calendar is "Aaron's Birthday". I'm keeping that day open for whatever grief brings.

I had lunch with Lorraine and Karin this afternoon. Karin was running late which offered Lorraine and I some one-on-one time. What Lorraine told me was truly enlightening. I had no idea about Lorraine's own experiences before today. She has never mentioned them. Funny how people tend to stay away from this subject until they hear that it's okay. "Aaron's Energy" opened the door for her to share with me.

Lorraine has had many connections through dreams and real-life experiences. She started by telling me about two close friends who passed away recently. Both of their widows began to find and collect dimes after their passing. Lorraine showed me photos of their dime collections. One was a photo of her friend surrounded by dimes his widow has collected. She ran out of room for all the dimes. Another was a large glass jar full of dimes.

Lorraine said that she has found dimes herself when thinking of her departed friends. She once found a dime on a forest path at exactly the moment that her friend was on her mind. Another time, she and her widowed friends were marvelling at the number of dimes they have found. When Lorraine went upstairs, there were two loose dimes by themselves on a bedroom dresser.

Lorraine is from Ireland. She is a radiant and loving person who puts her whole heart and mind into everything she does. She savours every moment. She is brave and unstoppable.

Irish mythology and folklore are tradition that have been spoken of and practiced there over generations. Lorraine is no stranger to it. When her grandmother passed, she sent Lorraine a dream message that she will make a television series about a girl who has the power to travel to other dimensions.

Lorraine said that she has a script about a doctor searching to communicate with his departed son. She believes that these film projects will deliver an important message about our connection to the spirit world. Also, she began to study quantum physics to authenticate the scripts she is working on.

Lorraine has creative genius. She understood "Aaron's Energy". She heard the physics in it. She said that she has found motivation to keep going with her projects since she read it.

Lorraine and I made a deeper connection because of "Aaron's Energy". So many people are responding with their stories. I feel the door opening more and more with each connection made.

Friday November 15, 2019.

Today is Aaron's birthday.

I've read that calendar firsts are particularly difficult for grieving people. To say that they're difficult is a gross understatement. I've been in fear of this day for good reason. The grief is hitting like a tsunami. The shock and disbelief are all back.

Jonathan wants to go to the cemetery today. I'm not sure if I can handle going there. I'm also not sure if I can handle not going. If I don't go, I won't be able to take it back. I don't want to add regrets on top of my grief. So, I'm going to go.

Aaron told me this morning that he is no longer bound by the chains of life's obligations. He said that all the energy tied to human survival is not of his world. He is free of those bindings. He said that human programming for survival is the driving force behind most thoughts, feelings, and actions. He has let go of the weight of that.

Aaron said that humans confuse progress with survival. He said, "Progress is not survival. People measure progress to convince themselves of their continued existence. Human measures and definitions of accomplishment, advancement, evolution, and progress are all tied to subjective reassurances. Definitions and measures are merely human creations to quell fears. The universe is not subjective."

Aaron said that our notions of progress are not really progress at all. Being open to the flow of energy of the universe, and seeking balance in it, is all that really matters. Imbalance with the flow of universal energy isn't survival, or progress. The universe doesn't "care". It is up to us to find balance. Have we? Look around the globe. How much has our "progress" really done to ensure our survival?

Arlene just called. Her father has been in the hospital for a couple of days. She told me he's going for tests today. He's very upset, and so is Arlene. She told me she heard her mother's voice say, "Dad will be okay." At that same moment, a red cardinal sculpture was brought in for consignment at her store. An orderly arrived to take Arlene's father for a test.

When he pulled the stretcher away, a dime was on the floor. Her niece saw a cardinal staring at her through her window from a snow-covered branch. Her brother found a shiny dime on his garage floor while he was getting into his car on the way to visit his father in the hospital. These events all occurred simultaneously. That's called universal synchronicity.

Jonathan and I went to the cemetery this afternoon. It was a dreadful, yet peaceful experience. The resurgence of shock and trauma made it difficult to stand up. But I found some strength in being there for Jonathan. He lost his big brother, and I am his mother. I heard Aaron say, "I'm with you wherever you go. Please go to places that provide you energy, peace, and balance, and I will be there." I will go to anyplace where I can be with Aaron.

Jonathan looked up to his big brother. He told me that he doesn't feel as safe without him. Jonathan didn't have an easy time growing up. Aaron looked after him. He took his role as older brother seriously.

Jonathan is smart, talented, and very resilient. He taught himself stop-motion animation at nine years old. He was making short movies with story arcs and posting them on YouTube. By fourteen he had taught himself computer 3D animation and was making video game characters. A career was born. Jonathan wanted to skip to the end, arguing that school was a basic waste of his time. This presented him with some challenges. Aaron worried over him. Fast-forward to today, and Jonathan is a video game creative artist and designer. Aaron is supportive of this career choice.

Sunday November 17, 2019.

Yesterday, we all got together for Zachary's birthday, which was on November 15th. The same day as Aaron's. Today is Zachary's girlfriend, Candice's birthday. Zach and Candice are a cute couple. Candice is from France. She is sweet and petite, pretty with brains, and a thick French accent. She learned English while doing her master's degree in art history. She has so much drive and ambition. She and Zach are similar that way. Zachary is an aerospace engineer with a master's in computer science. He is a math genius with wit and charm. Both are into computers in different ways. They compliment each other well.

We went to a nice restaurant for dinner and a pseudo-celebration. We made the best of it for Zach and Candice. But there was a heavy cloud of sadness hanging over the table and weighing down the occasion. It felt awful for so many reasons. I can imagine how hard this must be for Zach. He and Aaron celebrated the same birthday his whole life. That's not going to happen again. I couldn't bring myself to say happy birthday. It's too soon to be happy about anything. I feel like I'll never be happy again.

I can't imagine life without Aaron. I don't deserve to go on enjoying things when he can't. I have a choice, he doesn't. Despite all that has happened, and all Aaron has told me, it hasn't fully sunk in. We will never enjoy anything together again. This is how I feel without him on his birthday.

Aaron told me this evening that we do still share the energy of enjoyment. He is present and can connect with my energy. He says that the more I enjoy, the more enjoyment is available for him to share with me. He reminded me of how I felt whenever I saw him happy and enjoying anything. I remember how happy it made me to see him happy. He said that he feels the same way about me. "Mom, choose to be happy."

Monday November 18, 2019.

I asked Aaron if it's possible to predict the future. He said that it is. He said that it is pretty much equally not possible. Aaron said, "It's easier to predict what will happen when you see energy cycling back with itself. There aren't as many possibilities in that case."

I asked Aaron if it's possible to not exchange energy. He said, "No Mom. You're exchanging energy with every breath, thought, feeling, heartbeat, touch, sound, sight, and smell." He said that energy is in constant exchange with everything everywhere.

Tuesday November 19, 2019.

Back on November 8th, when I began hearing from other spirits and doubted it was real, I asked any of them to tell me about something I couldn't possibly already know. Remember when Ronda told me there is a box with her jewelry under her bed? I haven't said a word about this to anyone. I didn't want to do or say anything that might upset the ether. I wanted completely clear evidence of it, free of any possible kind of influence. Today, I got that.

This evening, I spoke with Cary. I inquired if I could ask him a question that might sound strange. "Sure, what is it?", he asked. I asked him if he keeps anything of Ronda's beside his bed. I said, "beside his bed", instead of under it, to prevent influencing his answer. He said, "No. Do you mean like a picture of her?" I said, "Anything." Then Cary said, "There was a box of her jewelry under the mattress." There it was. The proof that Ronda did speak to me from the other side.

Today, I played Canasta with my friends. It's the card game that's sweeping the nation. No wonder, it's fun. Alison told me she read some of "Aaron's Energy". She told me that she has seen her father in dreams. So did other members of her family. They made an agreement to share their dreams with each other every time their father appeared. Everyone in my Canasta group has shared their stories of connections with their loved ones who have passed. Each time we are together, we share our stories. We all want to keep those connections open. The veil is thinning.

I wasn't hearing as much from Aaron the past few days, though. I wondered if my energy wasn't compatible for exchange with him. I've been pretty depressed and crying since his birthday. I'm really missing him. The pain can be so agonizing, even physical.

A lot of people have offered to visit me. I think it's really considerate of them. I just haven't had enough energy to see everyone. There are only so many coffees and lunches a person can do in a week. I can't. Plus, there's so much that has to get done.

Aaron told me today that I shouldn't meet with anyone whose energy isn't compatible with mine. He said to let go of feeling obligated, guilty, or bad. He advised, "Remember Mom, let go of incompatible energy in order to connect with compatible energy. Be part of the flow."

Wednesday November 20, 2019.

I joined an online writing course. Today is the first day. We are writing about our grief to help cope with it. It's one of the best things that a grieving person can do for themselves. It's therapeutic. You don't have to be an accomplished author, or even a good one. Just write down your feelings.

Writing this journal has been helpful for me in so many ways so far. It has been good therapy. I'm also learning while I write. I feel connected with Aaron. Connecting with him gives me some relief from grieving. At the same time, I feel sad, depressed, and drained. I ache to have him back. Grief feelings are often mixed.

Maybe sharing with a group of grieving writers will be helpful. That's the objective. I'm going to include my writings here in my journal.

November 20, 2019. Who was the person I used to be?

I was Aaron's mother for nearly 32 years. Then one day, on September 22, 2019, I wasn't anymore. I don't know the person I am now. I just know that I'm not the person I used to be, and I never will be that person again. I guess I'll have to get to know this new person that I am, and that I'm becoming. I'm someone I didn't choose to be. I'm not ready to be this new person. I was ready to be a relaxed, retired, mother of four, grandmother of one. Back when I thought I had a choice; I was the mother of four. Now, I'm the mother trying to grieve the loss of my child, while trying to be supportive of his three siblings. How do I grieve and have the strength to be supportive at the same time? I have no idea what I'm doing. How can a lost and untethered person be supportive of anyone? I spend most of my time in a dense fog. Aaron helped me to know who I was. He was my eldest. Being his mother was everything. I've tried to take some baby steps toward an existence without Aaron physically here. It's been really tough. We were always there for each other. I hope he knows what a support he was for me.

This group seems to be helpful so far. We read each other's entries. We offer reassurance to each other. I have received some nice, supportive comments. I'm learning some writing skills while dealing with my grief. I'll stick with it.

November 21, 2019. What you don't know...

You don't know my loss. Not that I would want you to know it, so you'll know what to say. I wouldn't wish this on anyone. You should never know the loss of your child. I should never have known it, either. I don't really know the full extent of it yet, so I can't educate you. Like you, I thought I could understand this loss before it happened to me. I lost my mother before I lost my son. What you don't know, I didn't know too. You cannot compare loss. You can't understand it by comparison. So please, stop comparing. It isn't helping me. Oh, it's helping you. Sorry that my loss is making you uncomfortable.

Sorry that you don't know what to say. "Sorry for your loss" is all that you should say when you don't know what to say. Rambling on about yourself and your loss, asking probing questions, offering platitudes and pep talks, you don't know how unhelpful this is. It's hurtful. I know that's not your intention, but I don't know how to help you.

I don't even know the depth of my hurt. Please don't help me find it. I'll find it when I'm ready, not when you are. I have to find myself before I can find the extent of my pain. I don't know what comforts me, so how can you know. I can't help you.

I'm someone else now, someone I don't know. So, you don't know me. I used to know me. You used to know me. Now, I'm someone else. A huge part of me is lost. I'm adrift without my anchor, without my navigation, on an unknown course. I have no guidance for you.

I was pretty sure of things once. I felt secure. I felt a sense of where life was going. I prayed to a G-d I used to trust. I lived by the golden rule. I believed in "what goes around comes around". What went around to bring this around? I thought we were safe. I have no reassurances for you.

My journey has changed. I don't know where this goes. I just know everything is different. I don't know who I will be. What you don't know, is that I still care about you.

Members are stepping up with immediate support. I'm giving support to them in return. We all seem to get it. Keep writing.

November 22, 2019. How do I live in a landscape so vastly changed?

Hi again. It's me, Grief. Just cropped up again to let you know who's in charge here...and it's not you. Don't try to avoid me. Don't try to fight me. I've got bombs I can drop on you anytime without warning. I've got landmines too, so watch your step. I'm around every corner, ready to remind you that you can't get rid of me. So, you better get used to me. Your defenses are nothing against me. I am Grief.

That rose garden you planted that you thought would thrive forever, I trampled all over it. It's going to take a lot of years, a lot of water, and a lot of care to grow a new one. While you're trying to grow your new garden, I'll make sure you take a few steps back whenever you take steps forward. I've got wind, rain, hurricanes, tsunamis, and earthquakes. I can even block out the light. I am Grief.

This is my landscape since I lost my son two months ago. Words can be bombs. Good intentions are spotted with landmines. Life with my son went from beautiful to post-apocalyptic in an instant. I didn't know I was living on a fault line. I didn't know a tectonic shift was coming. The lights went out without warning. Grief is a tsunami. The earth swallowed me up.

Still in shock and traumatized, I don't know how to live in this nightmare. I still hope to wake up from it. Sometimes, I forget he's gone. Cruel reminders reveal the reality. I can't look forward to a new landscape without him in it. His absence stabs me. My wounds are still open. Groping around in the dark of my new landscape, I found some light here in writing, and sharing. It's a step forward.

Now, it's getting creative. We're developing our writing chops as we pour out our grief. It feels weirdly rewarding. I never had an opportunity to test this skill. I wish it had presented itself another way. Any other way.

November 23, 2019. I don't know what to do with my hands...

Aaron knew what to do with his hands. He was young, strong and creative. He was hands-on. He was giving. Giving of himself, and generous too. He was helpful. He helped set and clear the table at family dinners. He helped prepare and serve the meals. He used to tell me, "I'll clean up Mom, you made the dinner." He led our holiday dinners. Our first holidays without him were strange and surreal.

After the divorce, he became the man of our family. The eldest brother became a father figure to his younger siblings. That wasn't fair, but Aaron took it on with integrity, care, and love. He checked in with his brothers and sister often. We spoke every day and got together at least once or twice a week. If he saw that I was tired, he'd offer to rub my shoulders. He gave the best shoulder rubs.

He worked in construction in the summers. He was an artist and a craftsman. I can't do what he could do with his hands. He would come over and fix things that were broken, or in need of repair. He would climb a ladder when needed because he thought it was unsafe for me. He would help hang things, move things, paint things, and MacGyver things. But he's not here anymore to do those things.

I used to tell him that he'll make an amazing husband one day. My dream of my speech at his wedding was of all the bragging about him I would do in public. There was so much to brag about. Aaron had so many outstanding qualities. That day never came.

The things that I know to do with my hands mostly involve my children. The joy that I got from cooking and baking for them, selecting the perfect healthiest ingredients, setting the table, dialing their cell phone numbers, shopping together, choosing and wrapping their gifts, booking trips together, firing up the BBQ, shoveling the driveway for their cars, the list is endless. Aaron loved to lend a hand in everything "family". He was a family-loving person.

To say I miss him, sounds like an over-sized understatement. I'm lost without him. I know I have other children, but it doesn't feel like the same family anymore. Aaron was like the glue that held us all together. We'll have to figure it out. I'll have to figure out a new job for these hands.

Saturday November 23, 2019.

While preoccupied with grief writing and feeling awfully depressed, I haven't connected as often with Aaron. I think my energy has turned to my writing, and on the writings of the others in my group. On the one hand, I feel that it's helpful to hear stories in common. But on the other hand, I'm feeling depressed by reading so many sad stories all day long.

Aaron has reminded me that he's still present and is never leaving me. He knows that my writing is making me miss him terribly. So, I took a break from it to clean up my office. It looks more like a cluttered storage unit than an office. It's full of boxes of my mother's things, and now Aaron's. It's painful and comforting to be surrounded by their stuff.

Once I got through enough mess in the closet to see the floor, a shiny dime lay there peering up at me. It's where I was planning to put my mother's boxes. I picked up the dime and held it to my heart for a while before putting it in the bowl with my collection.

I opened a box, and on the top of the box was an envelope with a picture of a large red cardinal on the front. I felt both Aaron and my mother were there with me, letting me know that it was a good idea to make room to keep the things that belonged to them. Their energy is still in those things. I keep them with me this way.

Sunday November 24, 2019.

We went to the cottage again today. I anticipate hearing from Aaron there, far away from the noise of the city and the interference of life. I found it really hard this time. I cried a lot. Aaron reminded me that it's normal to be sad. He's around me when I'm sad too.

While in a hardware store, I wondered if he was with me, and thinking this was a silly place to wonder that. As I had that thought, I spotted a red cardinal figurine on a shelf. Then I spotted another and another. Of all places, there were a bunch of cardinal figurines in the hardware store. I had to buy one to take home with me. Every time I see it, I recall that Aaron was with me when I bought it.

Souvenir Cardinal

I often hear people say, "There's no such thing as coincidence." I had to ask Aaron about this. "Coincidence occurs constantly.", he said. "Some events appear as chance to humans. Coincidence, serendipity, and luck (good or bad) are not fully explainable in human terms. Humans like to attach value to everything. Universal value is in the flow."

When we arrived at the cottage, I lit a Memory Candle. I keep Memory Candles lit at home. I brought a one-day candle. But it stayed lit the whole two-and-a-half days that we were there. Aaron's energy was in it.

Saturday November 30, 2019.

I took a break from the writing course again today. Aaron said that my energy has been difficult the last few days. I've been really depressed and crying a lot. I'm wondering if it was too early for me to be part of this group. Since I started the daily group writing, I've been slipping deeper into depression.

I am reading multiple daily entries from other grievers. I write daily according to the prompts that are emailed to the group. I understand how this is supposed to be helpful.

Actually, I can't seem to relate to most of the group. The only ones I can really relate to are those who have lost children. There's about five of us in this group of at least twenty-five members. Although we all have grief in common, we are all at different points with different types of loss. It's overwhelmingly depressing to read about this much grief every day.

Interestingly though, I heard more from Aaron today. He said that my energy today was easier to connect with. Maybe the break is helping. I also heard from my mother and Cindy's father. I actually hear him in his voice with his Hungarian accent. I asked them both this time if we really are relatives. Cindy's father said that he and my mother are distant cousins on her mother's side and his father's side. My mother said that Cindy's father keeps telling her they're cousins. She said they share some distant relative from Hungary. She says that he is always making her laugh with his humour and positive attitude. She was always my father's straight man. My father could have been a stand-up comedian.

Everybody loves my father. He is off-the-cuff witty and super funny. He had smouldering good looks when he was a young man. My parents looked like a golden-era Hollywood couple. My father has an intelligent, dry sense of humour. He always draws a crowd. People can't wait to hear what he'll say next. He and his brothers are a comedy team. Family get-togethers are always full of laughter. He's got his serious side, though. He served in three wars during his career in the armed forces.

He saw a lot of tragedy. His humour probably helped him get through all of that. I never saw him so sad as when he lost my mother, and then again when he lost Aaron.

Arlene visited me today. When she arrived, she told me that she heard from Aaron on her way to my house. He told her to tell me to stop the writing course for now. It's putting me in too much of a fog, which makes it harder for him to connect. While Arlene and I were talking, she saw Aaron standing beside me.

Aaron said, "The reason we exist is because the energy of the universe made us. While we are alive, we need to learn how to connect with the flow by helping other people, animals, and everyone around us. In this way, we work with the whole universe." Then, he added, "That's all we really need to know."

Tuesday December 3, 2019.

We decided that a vacation in the sun might do us some good. Here in Florida, I'm hoping that I'll feel better. The weather has not disappointed us. It's sunny and warm in Miami in December. We've been outside every day. There's a nice pool with a patio bar and restaurant at our hotel. The beach out front looks breath-taking. Daily walks on the beach have been good for fitness, and for taking the weight off of my grief.

A small sandpiper followed us along the beach on our walk today. It broke from its group to stick with us. My first thought was that Aaron sent the little bird to see us. I asked him, "Why send birds?" He said that animal energy is in flow with universal energy. "Animals are uncomplicated and so much easier to connect with. Their eyes are our eyes, their ears are our ears, their senses are our senses. Animal brains are much quieter than humans. Young human children are easier to connect with as well."

We often hear stories of young children relating "past life" experiences. These phenomena occur when energies are connected across the veil, and the child can report some memories from another time or generation.

I captured a photo of the little fellow.

Sandpiper

December 3, 2019. What would it take?

In order to feel safe within my pain, it would take trust. I don't trust myself enough yet to find trust in others.

In order to find strength inside my pain, it would take balance. I'm not balanced enough yet to feel strong.

In order to soften into my pain, it would take comfort. Perhaps in time, I will grant myself some comfort, but I'm not yet deserving.

In order to find love within my pain, it would take knowing love. I have known great and endless love, and therefore I have found it.

It seems like the writing course isn't as depressing while I'm on vacation. I'm feeling better and back at it.

December 3, 2019. A Fractured Fairy Tale

A crystal ball sits atop a pedestal on a shelf. Inside it stands a delicate porcelain fairy with gossamer wings, a golden crown and shimmering chiffon dress. In her raised hand she holds her sparkling magic wand. Her world inside her crystal ball is a beautiful fairy tale of her creation. At her feet, her children and puppies play. They are surrounded by flowers on rolling hills sprinkled with glitter. Her world is gleaming with beauty. It's perfect and happy, bright, and sunny. Her heart is filled with happiness and love. It's safe inside her crystal ball. Then one day, a sharp crack splinters the globe.

Outside her crystal ball exists another world. The inhabitants there are mostly dark and cumbersome. Occasionally, her perfect world is darkened by the shadows of those who exist on the other side. They want to seep into her world. Their presence makes the fairy uneasy. They try to find a way into her world. They've shaken it. They've turned it upside down. They call out to her. They attempt to lure her with strange language. They weaken her. She feels defenceless. She wishes they would just go away and leave her alone. She tries to repair the crack in the crystal, but her powers fail her. Her magic wand is useless. She cowers and shies away from their invitations. She curls up under her wings and waits for the darkness to pass. She prays that the light will return her powers, and she will create herself a new world.

Thursday December 5, 2019.

This vacation has been doing me some good. I'm able to relax a bit and find some peaceful moments. I have even caught up on the whole writing course. I've made more than one entry on some days.

December 5, 2019. Your world is entirely new, now.

Aaron, I was struggling with this one, because it's so new. Today, I can tell you that every single thing, every molecule, atom, and particle, of this place has changed since you left, despite that everything still looks the same. Love Forever, Mom

December 5, 2019. I didn't know...

What stands out the most to me since I started is that I have a supportive community holding my hand as I write. Through reading and writing, the weight of my pain gets a bit lighter by sharing. This is not the life I ever wanted, or ever wished on anyone. But I am grateful to be not alone.

December 5, 2019. What is the condition of my heart?

I visualize my actual heart. It's held together with chains and heavy locks to keep it together. It's covered in bruises. Sometimes it beats. Sometimes it doesn't. The locks and chains are so heavy. They weigh a ton. My poor little heart is barely visible behind them. There are a few band-aids trying to stop the blood spilling out. Some clots are forming to keep the blood inside. My heart struggles to keep going.

It manages to muster up some beats for my children and my grandchild because it knows it still has love inside.

Friday December 6, 2019. I had a dream last night about Catherine. She was stealing the show in a stage play with her witty rendition of a song. It was a duet. She was dressed in a white dress and pumps. She looked like an angel. She was funny. I was in the audience laughing and applauding. When I woke up, I saw a text from Catherine that said she was thinking of me. She sent it in the middle of the night. Maybe during my dream about her.

December 6, 2019. Grief is everywhere.

Clenched fists. Furrowed brow. Watery eyes. Frowning mouth. Clamped jaw. Stiff joints. Dry throat. Knotted stomach. Tightened chest. Shallow breathing. Foggy brain.

Grief is oozing from every pore out into the world. Rippling from the inside out. Floating through space and time. Bounding and rebounding. Permeating and penetrating everything.

Grief has its own dimension. It enters and exits whenever it wants. It has gravity. It obeys and disobeys. It has order but is lawless.

Grief has weight and mass. It is dense and heavy. It has its own energy. It flows inward and outward, back, and forth like the tide. Grief is a reminder to remember.

Grief has volume. It is large and small. It is loud and quiet. It has words but is sometimes unspoken. Its silence is engulfing. Its music is sad.

Grief has darkness but is also enlightening. It can hide in the shadows. Or it can turn on the lights. It can flash like a camera. It has its own library of photos and images.

Grief burns with its own fire. It freezes with the coldest cold.

Every object, every sight, every sound, every smell, every thought, and feeling holds grief within it. Grief is everywhere.

Tonight, in the bottom of a pocket, I found a dime wrapped in a gas station receipt from Peterborough. We just happened to be talking about buying a cottage near there. I have been thinking about getting a cottage for years. The kids would love one. I've just been too scared to do it alone.

Cottages are so much work, and I don't have any experience. I love Anthony's cottage. The kids love it too. But it's a three-hour drive to get there. The kids don't come often. What is this dime trying to tell me? Get the cottage.

December 8, 2019. I want to remember...I want to forget

This is a hard one. I could write a book on all I want to remember about my son. I want to remember every minute of his life. I want to forget that he's gone. I could write another similar book about my mother.

My mother passed away this May, two days before Mother's Day. My son's passing in September, just a few months later, has made me all but forget my mother's.

I want to remember my son's birth. He was my first. I remember no greater joy. He was so bright and wonderful. He was a loving brother to his three younger siblings. We

84

had a close mother-son relationship. He was wise beyond his years. He was intelligent and witty. He was always kind and considerate. He was generous, warm, and loving. When he was not yet three years old, I was tying his shoes for preschool and some coins fell from my pocket. He quickly scooped them up. He cried so hard when I told him he couldn't take coins to school. Since I could already reason with him, he could keep them in his pocket if he didn't take them out. Later that morning, the principal called. I had visions that some kid had choked on one of my son's coins. I timidly answered the phone. She told me that he had given each of his classmates a coin and told them to put theirs in the charity box. She had never seen a child so young do something like that. I was so proud of my son. This was the kind of person he remained his whole life. I have told this story many times. I want to remember it.

I want to forget the trauma when the police came to my house to tell me about my son's fatal accident.

I want to remember my mother's life, and her intelligence, class, and beauty. She was brave and accomplished. She was a successful businesswoman and mother. She was no nonsense. She got all the answers on Jeopardy, her favourite show. I was always inspired by my mother to be the best person I could be. She had such wisdom and strength. She lived a long and healthy life. She was never sick until she was diagnosed with leukaemia. I thought she would beat it because she was always the strong one. Everyone, even her doctor thought she was doing well with her chemotherapy. But septicaemia took her life.

I want to forget the trauma of being present when my mother was taken off life support. The doctor thought I could handle it because I was a critical care nurse and had so much experience. I thought I could handle it too. But I was wrong. It was very traumatic for me. I was just

beginning to feel a bit better, when I was told the tragic
news about my son.

I want to remember their lives but forget that they're gone.

December 10, 2019. A Shift in Grief

Every night I go to bed grieving, and every morning I wake
up grieving. At home, I am surrounded by memories of my
son. I thought a vacation would shift my grief.

Maybe taking sometime away would help. Maybe relaxing
in the sun would take my mind somewhere else for a bit of
a break. I found out that you can't take a vacation from
grief. It goes with you. I have had momentary lapses while
on my vacation. But they are split-second. Even that in
those fleeting moments, I feel pulled back to my grief
fearful of losing my memories.

Tuesday December 10, 2019.

I've been struggling with my grief while on vacation. It's
hard to know what to do. Maybe I can create some
distractions from it. I asked Aaron if we have a purpose
while are in our human form. He said, "Our purpose is to fit
with the universal flow of energy. Any way we can find that
fit in life, whatever we do to achieve it, serves our purpose.
We must use our bodies while we are in them for this
purpose, too."

Aaron said that there is no pre-set purpose for life. "Our
energy of spirit randomly connects with our energy of
bodily matter. Our bodies randomly came to be, as did
every form of matter. We are part of the energy flowing
through the universe. We must live within the flow and

balance. You could say in retrospect that we planned our existences for a reason. But prospect and retrospect are context dependent constructs that don't fit here like they do there. Everyone finds their fit differently as a part of the whole. We are each unique, but we all come from the same source."

Aaron said that people must find a way toward self-compatibility. "People who are in energy struggles with themselves will inevitably be in energy struggles with other people. This is not sustainable. Everyone has the option to redirect their energy to more compatible exchanges with themselves, which will result in compatible exchanges with others."

Grief feels like a constant energy struggle. Perhaps it interferes with my connection with Aaron. Going for walks has been helping lift the grief. It really is beautiful here. I've always liked Christmastime in Florida. The palm trees decorated with twinkling lights look so magical. I can feel Aaron here in the magic.

Wednesday December 11, 2019.

It's been one of those days when everyone seems aggravated, rude, and impatient. People can be so inconsiderate. What has happened to the world? Kindness shouldn't be so difficult. But it seems that there are so many angry, unhappy people.

The Golden Rule. It is addressed in every religion on earth. But, in Judaism, why is it addressed in the negative? Aaron said, "Judaism recognises the necessity of this concept: Do not do unto others what you know is harmful to you. It is absolutely essential to the balance of energy."

He added, "Christianity turned it around into: Do unto others as you would have them do unto you. The Christian interpretation is more vast, and less specific. People have a hard time setting limits on their expectations. What would they have others do unto them? The options are endless."

He went on to say, "Universal balance is of utmost importance. I like the logic of Judaism. People have a short, and limited list of what they know is harmful to themselves. They feel sure of what they don't want. But they find it hard to pinpoint what they do want. So, we have an innate internal compass, no thinking required." In other words, kindness is already born in us.

Aaron points out that he is no longer partial to any religion. His references to Judaism make it easier for him to explain the unexplainable to me. It's a way for us to relate to each other. That is what is most important. "The purpose of all religion should be to help people relate with themselves, each other, and the universe."

December 11, 2019. I Remember...

I remember my son's grandmother, and the loving relationship they had. She passed away when he was only 8 years old. She was so gentle and kind. She was an artist and environmentalist, way before it became a movement. Aaron was her first grandchild. She loved to teach him about nature and art, and to see art in nature. One day, when Aaron was 3 years old, he excitedly showed me an orange maple leaf he and his grandmother found on a walk together. It was a discovery for him. She showed him to look deeply at the intricate details of the leaf. He showed me all of the veins, colours, shades, and markings of the leaf. He told me about its lifecycle, what kind of tree it started from, and why its colour had changed, and it fell to the ground. Aaron would sit on his grandmother's knee while she read stories to him or made up her own fascinating stories for him. She was gone way too young way too soon. I probably didn't realize the impact of her loss on such a young child. But I saw the impact of losing her to the whole family over the years. After all these years, I have learned of the long-term impact of loss. I still miss her. I will always miss him. I hope they are reunited in their new existence.

December 11, 2019. What has been outgrown?

Losing my child forced me to outgrow my delusion that being a good person, trying to do my best as a mother, and being there for my kids would keep them safe and healthy. My assumption that my children would all outlive me is now disillusion. These beliefs have been replaced with pain, heartbreak, disappointment, and failure. I'll hold on to who I am as a mother for my surviving children, but my belief in my capacity and impact has been forever abandoned.

December 14, 2019. How would you love me in this?

I am your son, and I always will be. Our love is eternal. I will love you through everything forever. Our connection never ends. We have always been together. I am still here in the energy around you, and within your heart and mind. I am part of you, and you are part of me. My energy is always present.

We are flowing together. I feel your feelings. I am always here to comfort you when you need me. When you're feeling pain, I send you signals of my presence to remind you that I'm around. I know those signals are comforting for you, because I feel your pain ease when you see and hear them. I love you in this as I love you in everything.

Sunday December 15, 2019.

My sister and her boyfriend came to visit us for a couple of days. They stayed at the same hotel as us. They drove across Florida. It was good for me that they came. We had a nice, relaxing time together.

Leah and I went for walks on the beach every day during their stay. We got a lot of chatting in too. She made a comment, "You can never get away from someone you've had children with." Immediately, I heard Aaron add, "You can't get away from anyone you've shared existence with, because they have always been there and always will be." I didn't tell Leah what Aaron said, or that I could hear him. But he was definitely part of our conversation. His point was well taken.

December 15, 2019. Breath

I think about breathing a lot. Most people aren't conscious of it. It's automatic. But I have a chronic problem with my lungs. I have to remember to breath deeper. My breathing has been too shallow recently. Sometimes the space between breaths has been so long, I have time to think about stopping altogether and not restarting. That kind of thinking creates an internal argument. I give into that argument every time and take the next breath. There's a life in the space between breaths. There are possibilities. Somewhere inside me there's an urge to go on. Maybe there are things I still need to do, questions I need answered. Maybe I'll just give in to the mystery of life.

December 15, 2019. Don't think. Just write

I don't wake up happy. I don't have my heart back. I am ambushed by grief every day. It seems that the work of grief will never be done, and I will never heal. But I have seen the invisible form of my son, and I do believe he is waiting for me to join him when my time comes.

Monday December 16, 2019.

Back in Toronto. There's snow on the ground, and the holidays are coming up soon. I feel like I can't take it. The grief is overpowering. The disbelief is crippling me yet again. I'm guessing this is how it will always be.

Thursday December 19, 2019.

The holidays are around the corner. This will be the first Hanukkah that Aaron won't be here to light the Menorah. He loved to take the lead at holidays. Family, faith, and food abounded at our house. Aaron always came over early to help prepare the meal and set the table. He took such great care. He stayed after to help with clean up, too. This holiday season, there won't be a dinner. There won't be any celebration. No one feels like celebrating.

I miss Aaron so much every day, but it seems that I miss him more now. I'm having trouble enjoying anything, and I'm not enjoying the holidays either. I'll try to think of them as comforting, since that seems to work sometimes. But sometimes, nothing works to ease the stabbing pain. I just have to try to breathe through it.

This morning, I wondered, *"What does it all mean, anyway."* I feel lost without Aaron. What does life really mean? Aaron answered my question right away, "You give meaning to life, Mom. Your life's meaning is what you make it."

Sunday December 22, 2019.

Through a window I saw the ivy leaves on our next-door neighbour's house rustling. It's an unusually warm day for December. I went to the window to take a closer look. All of a sudden, a bright red cardinal flew out of the ivy. In my surprise, I said, "Aaron!"

This morning I went to a class at my synagogue about Hanukkah miracles. Aaron was there with me and was interrupting the teacher. "This class is over-simplified, and the teacher knows it." He kept talking to me as the teacher lectured. The teacher said that miracles are not naturally occurring phenomena. They occur to let us know HaShem is an all-powerful creator who can alter nature.

"HaShem" literally means "The Name" in Hebrew. One is not allowed to utter God's name unless for Sabbath prayer. Any other mention of it would be in vain, which is high on the Ten Commandments of what not to do.

Aaron said, "It's plain false. People define natural, unexplained phenomena as miracles." He said that there is a lot to nature that we are unable to perceive. "Nature is always in balance. People lack the capacity to understand how it all works itself out."

Tonight, we will light the first candle for Hanukkah. Aaron loved this holiday, all eight nights of it. He lit our Menorah. Now, Aaron is the light. He is the Shamash, the candle that is used to light the eight others. We will continue with the tradition for him, and to think of him as our guiding light. Jonathan offered to step in and light the Menorah for Aaron. I feel his absence, yet I also feel his presence.

Jonathan lit the Menorah. We said blessings, and sang "Maoz Tzur", "Rock of Ages". It's a song about miracles that is sung at Hanukkah. We discussed what the blessings and the song mean. I can't explain things the way Aaron could. Now I know that he was helping me in class this morning for tonight's discussion. So much is occurring in synchrony.

Later tonight, I felt worse about Aaron's absence. I began thinking that nothing really matters anymore. It doesn't matter if I don't wake up in the morning. Losing a child can come with terrible feelings like this. Aaron said, "Stay where you are, Mom. It matters now. You will be here with me one day, and you won't notice the time passed. The length of time we spend in human form is not measured separately from our spiritual existence. It is perceived differently. The time we spent in different forms will seem relatively insignificant when we are together again."

Monday December 23, 2019.

Shelby and Caleb moved into a new apartment on the weekend. Hopefully, this will be a better life for my daughter and grandson. It's a beautiful apartment, and we've enjoyed furnishing and decorating it. Caleb has his own room. It's just the right size for a five-year-old boy, and all of his pets and paraphernalia.

Shelby is a young single mom on her own with Caleb. It's hard. I'm trying to be as supportive of them as possible. Being supportive of my children after losing one of them is an emotional challenge. I'm still their parent and I have to be strong for them, regardless of how weak I feel.

We had a discussion about her responsibilities in her new living arrangements. Shelby can be very bottled up. I felt that she wasn't being totally honest with me. It's hard to know because she doesn't say much. I think "Aaron's Energy" might help her learn to get into better relationships. As soon as I had that thought, I heard Aaron say, "Some of what she's saying isn't true." He wouldn't tell me which was which.

Tonight, I began reading "Beyond Weird: Why Everything You Thought You Knew about Quantum Physics Is Different", by Philip Ball[8]. Lorraine recommended the book. It's one of the physics books she's reading for her film prep.

The author explains that everything we think of as real in our world is merely analogy that serves our perceptions, while the whole of reality exists beyond our grasp. I wouldn't call quantum physics easy reading, but you don't need to be a physicist to understand this book.

So much of what Aaron has been telling me about energy and the universe I am reading in a book about physics. The parallels between Aaron's messages and the information in this book are remarkable.

---

[8] "Beyond Weird: Why Everything You Thought You Knew about Quantum Physics Is Different", by Philip Ball, October 18, 2018 University of Chicago Press

Friday December 27, 2019.

Anthony made a rhubarb pie this afternoon. Its delicious aroma wafted through the whole house. I felt that Aaron would have loved to have a piece of that pie, and it made me sad that he couldn't. Aaron told me, "I can smell the pie, Mom."

He said that he detects pleasant aromas like he sees pleasant sights. In a way, he "feels" the scent of things by the energy their molecules emit, and by his connection with the receptor. In this case, my nose is the receptor. He said that Anthony's pie smelled amazing, and he never even liked rhubarb.

Saturday December 28, 2019.

I spent the week with a bad cold. Being sick and grieving are a bad brew. I'm so congested that whenever I cry my airway gets completely obstructed. It's not a good visual. I heard from Aaron here and there, mostly reassuring me that he is always nearby.

This evening as I got undressed for bed, I thought about whether or not Aaron was there. Maybe he didn't want to be nearby me as I got washed and changed. Aaron told me that his energy is always around. He said that he can "see" everything in my world. He said that the concerns and embarrassments of human life are not part of his world. He understands what is necessary to deal with in human form.

Monday December 30, 2019.

Arlene and her husband came over for dinner. It was so nice to spend time with them talking about experiences without the distractions of a crowd. We've shared the ups and downs of life for many years now. Arlene told me privately that she saw Aaron standing behind me at the table. She said that she didn't mention it at dinner because she knows that not everyone believes in spirit visits. She said that Aaron had his hand on my shoulder as if to say that he is watching over and protecting me. That's my Aaron for sure.

As I watch the snowflakes falling

Existing from a universal elemental collision

Each one unique and special

In icy geometric perfection

They are all different yet similar

Alone yet together

Each on their quiet journeys

Eventually meeting where they land

Some to stay together for a while

Some to take to the wind

And find another place or another form

I slip into a reverie

Under the peaceful blanket of snow

A momentary feeling of warmth

Of the perfection of creation

The comfort of the universe

But I suddenly awaken to the shiver of my isolation

Surrounded by a frozen blanket

As I face the chill of loneliness. Camille Dan 2019

Thursday January 2, 2020.

New Year's Eve and New Year's Day came and went. No celebrating or watching the ball drop. No ringing in the new. I wanted the old back. I went to bed early. Facing a new year and a new decade without Aaron made the grief even more unbearable than I thought possible.

Last night as I sat reading, I heard Aaron calling my name. "Mom...Mom...Mom...Moooooom!" He sounded lost, or if something was wrong, but he didn't tell me what it was. I was scared. I told him I'm always here for him. He told me that he's always here for me.

In "Beyond Weird..." Philip Ball writes about the wave/particle properties of light and electrons. In a word, "physics". He refers to a classic experiment in quantum mechanics that demonstrates our lack of ability to fully understand how the universe works. It's called the quantum double-slit experiment. In it, electrons are shot through two slits, cut beside each other into a cardboard card, on to a metal receiving wall. The electrons land in a characteristic diffraction pattern on the metal wall as waves of them interfere with each other on their paths. So, electrons behave like particles first, and then they behave like waves.

In an attempt to see if the slits had some effect on the electrons to cause this particle-wave transition, a detection device is put on one of the slits. With the detection device on, no electrons appear to pass through that slit. When the device was turned off, the electrons return to their previous pattern.

This experiment has been repeated countless times yielding exactly the same results. The electrons don't pass through the slit with the detector on. How do the electrons "know" when the detector is turned off or on? There's no known answer to that.

Aaron told me, "This is what I've been talking about, Mom. Human beings can only measure universal phenomena to the extent of their physical senses. Human made measures are merely reflective of what is present. For example, energy in the form of heat. Heat is a form of energy, and also a reflective form of it. So, heat can or cannot be detected and measured. The full inherent properties of energy are not measurable by human beings." He said that what we are capable of sensing while in the human state is all we really need to know during life. Universal knowledge will come when we are where he is.

I had lunch with Alison today. She told me a story about an encounter with a deer she had when she was begging to make contact with her father. He passed away many years ago. She was really missing him while on a nature walk. When she looked up, there stood a male deer with tall antlers staring at her. She was with some friends who also had an encounter with deer when their father passed away last year. Alison's father, their father, and a cousin's father were best friends. The other two fathers had passed a long time before. When the third one lay dying, his son spotted two deer outside his window. His father passed, and when he looked out the window, he saw three deer. He said he knew this was a sign that his father had reunited with his two best friends. I told Alison about what Aaron told me. Animals can act as eyes and ears for the departed.

Friday January 3, 2020.

Aaron told me that the reason he is able to continue connecting with me is because I'm open to it. He said that spirit energy is always present and available. He said that most souls cannot stay with their surviving loved ones for long because they do not maintain the energy balance necessary to do so. "For whatever their reason, whether their grief is too profound, or they are too busy with life's distractions, they make themselves difficult for us to connect with." Aaron often reminds me how to control my complicated emotions and distractions so that we can make connections. I practice with him often so that he stays nearby.

Monday January 6, 2020.

It snowed last night. After a busy day, visiting with Zach and Candice, shopping for items for Shelby's new apartment, and then returning to Zach's to install a new light switch, it was comforting to sit and watch the quiet snow fall.

This morning when I woke up, the feeling of missing Aaron was intense. I began to have those *"he's gone and never coming back"* thoughts again. Those thoughts always make me cry. I heard Aaron say that he is not gone, I just can't see him.

I cried more thinking that I've probably been making this all up in my head the whole time. I begged Aaron to tell me that he's truly present. Right at that moment, I heard a chirping sound outside the window behind me. I looked out and saw a bright red cardinal atop my snow-capped fence, chirping gently. It looked at me when I moved the curtains to see it, but it didn't fly away. It wasn't scared. It stayed and looked right at me for a minute first. It was Aaron at the right moment looking at me through the bird's eyes.

Monday January 13, 2020.

I asked Aaron this week if he is able to change outcomes. He said that he cannot change past events, only feelings about them, but might have some influence over future events. He said, "Mom, you're asking questions that aren't easy to answer. This is very intricate because of the complexity of the universe. Simply put, energy flows through everything, and people can't fully observe how it works. Large scale variations in flow can happen but having influence over them implies a desire for change. Energy doesn't desire anything. It naturally goes to where it is needed for balance. In other words, it doesn't want anything in the way people do." He said that where he is there is no desire or want.

Tuesday January 14, 2020.

As I drove home from my father's after taking him for a tumour removal, the traffic was diverted to Yonge Street. I don't like taking this route. It goes by many places that Aaron and I used to go. His apartment building is near here, and I had to drive past it. It's where Aaron's fatal accident happened. I've been able to avoid passing by here until now.

I started to cry, not a good thing while behind the wheel, and I asked Aaron if he could see where I was. The traffic suddenly came to a stop. I turned my head to see a store that sold bird food. It had a large poster of a red cardinal in its front window. Aaron must have heard me and showed me a sign. If the traffic hadn't stopped, I would have driven right by never seeing it.

All of a sudden, I heard Shirley's voice out of nowhere. She told me Marissa will get pregnant in 2020. I was so excited.

I wanted to tell Arlene what her mother just told me, but I knew how upset she would be if it didn't happen. So, I didn't tell her.

Wednesday January 15, 2020.

Spirits do not speak ill of others. They don't tell you much about other people's lives, either. If they ever do, it is only about something helpful, or useful to promote balance. If you don't need to be included, or involved, they let you know by not answering your questions. In other words, spirits don't gossip, and they don't triangulate.

If knowing something will help you, they will let you know. Aaron tells me often, "I'm always available to be helpful, Mom." I think they know best. Where Aaron is, they have a wide view from above. They can see the whole picture, as we only see a small part through a narrow lens.

Monday January 20, 2020.

While out for a walk with Cindy today, she asked me if I've heard from her father lately. She asked me to ask him if things will be ok. Her father answered me in his voice that things will be ok, and to tell Cindy to keep trying to find balance within herself.

Cindy told me she wishes to hear her father. We will arrange a quiet, relaxing time together, and I will show her how. I know she will hear him when she gets how to make the connection.

Wednesday January 22, 2020.

Sinking further into sadness and depression again. Grief seems to cycle like this. Today is the four-month mark since Aaron passed. I'm still in shock and disbelief, and depression is setting in deep.

I have already learned that physical activity improves how I feel. I increased my fitness sessions with my trainer to three times per week. I have less than zero motivation to do anything these days. Nor do I wake up any mornings with an impulse to lift weights or repeat crunches and knee-drivers until I'm blue in the face. But if it's recorded in my calendar to do this with my trainer, I begrudgingly find a way to push myself through. At the end of each workout, I always feel better than I did at the beginning.

I can play tennis, too. I went to the club for some court time in a clinic today to get some exercise. My luck, an aggressive player showed up. She was right out of the cast of "Mean Girls". She even had the "hair flip" mastered. Sigh, I really don't need this right now.

After a few rounds of aggressive play, she deliberately slammed a shot at close range directly at the net player on my side. It missed her, but I saw the intention to hit her in Mean Girl's face. I stopped playing, put up my hand and said, "I'm out." I walked off the court and left the building. It felt so good to stand up for my feelings and to do what I needed to take care of myself. I'm learning balance. Thank you, Aaron.

Jonathan, Anthony, and I went to see a movie this evening called, "Jumanji". It's an action-adventure, comedy starring Dwayne Johnson and Kevin Hart. I like them. I thought a good comedy would provide me a distraction. In one scene, a character who is dying of cancer chooses to remain permanently as his Avatar in the Jumanji video game instead of returning to himself in real life. His Avatar is a winged horse. Upon announcing his decision, he flies off into the sky.

Of course, it was emotionally wrenching for me, and I started to cry. All at once, I had a visceral feeling of Aaron's presence in the seat next to mine. I asked Aaron if he was with me watching the movie. He said that he was there, and that he doesn't "see" the movie the way I do, but he feels it. He can feel my feelings about it. It's kind of like we're watching the movie together through my eyes.

Thursday January 23, 2020.

Cindy and I went out for dinner to one of our favourite French restaurants tonight. I heard a lot from her father during our meal. He was interrupting our conversation with his own input. He told me when he thought something Cindy said was good, and he gave his advice when he thought it was helpful. He told me to tell Cindy that she needs to let things go that aren't helping her energy. So, I did. We clinked our wine glasses and cried.

Cindy really misses her father. I understand how that feels. He was a great dad and a great human being. I am determined to get them talking to each other.

Friday January 24, 2020.

We came to Miami to celebrate Candice and Zachary's recent engagement. Her parents have stopped over on their flight back home to France from Nicaragua. I say, celebrate, even though I'm not really up to celebrations. Family events are extra hard without Aaron. He reminds me often that he's not absent. But I would rather he was physically present if I could have things my way. I miss his bear hugs.

Monday January 27, 2020.

It's nice to see Candice's parents. They are lovely and down-to-earth. The kids are so happy. I'm happy for them. We celebrated with a big dinner at one of Miami's finest restaurants. Courses of gourmet food and wine. One of those see-and-be-seen places with Michelin Stars. To me it was crowded and loud. That meant for strained conversation across the big table. Anyway, I was okay with the noise given my torn feelings. It's weird to feel happy and heartbroken at the same time. There's nothing I can do to change that. So, there I was in sad/happy mode again.

Tuesday January 28, 2020.

Anthony and I drove across Florida today to spend a few days in Clearwater. Jonathan flew down to Tampa to meet us. We picked him up at the airport, and we all met up with Leah and Jack at their house. They live year-round in this sunny paradise.

It's been a long time since I've visited the Gulf side of Florida. I used to take the kids down here for the white-powder sand beaches, warm gulf water, multiple amusement parks, aquariums, museums, and the sun. I know I sound like a tourist ad, but there's all that here and more. Of course, being here has drawn up memories of young Aaron.

Back in March of 2019 Jonathan, Anthony and I went on a road trip to Key West. It's such a charmingly lazy place with its "Jimmy Buffet" vibe. We took the scenic route from one key to the next across the Florida Archipelago from Miami. While there, we toured the town and Hemingway's house. We made sure to enjoy a piece or two of key lime pie.

Tonight, I was by myself at the hotel getting ready for bed, and Aaron spoke to me. He told me, "Don't get too upset, or caught up with the passing of time, Mom. Nothing in the physical world stays permanently in one state. The only thing that is permanent in the universe is energy. Everything that you can see, no matter how solid it appears, is coming apart at different rates. Look at the granite counter, that box of Kleenex, and the water in the gulf. Look at yourself in the mirror. All of these things eventually come apart. Some solid objects, whether man-made or natural, take a very, very long to disintegrate. Other objects, especially organic, decompose fairly quickly in comparison." Aaron reminded me not to worry, "When we are together again, it won't feel like it's been for very long. It only feels like we're apart for a long time because you can't be fully conscious of my present energy."

Friday February 7, 2020.

Yesterday, the assisted living home called me about my father. They said he needs a hospital bed. I spoke with my father about it. He said that he feels too weak to walk. He is 93 years old, and not in good health. I'm concerned. My father's health hasn't been good for years. He's become increasingly frail since my mother died. My mother was his caregiver. That's true love.

My mother told me that she doesn't want him to come where she is yet. That was a surprise. Now she's telling me not to write what she just said. She said, "Camille, I'm not ready for him, and he's not ready to go yet." Today on Facebook, I saw a video post by Ziad Masri called, "This Will

105

Change Your Life"[9]. Ziad Masri is the author of, "Reality Unveiled: The Hidden Keys of Existence That Will Transform Your Life (and the World)"[10].

Ziad was an entrepreneur who set out on a 15-year journey of self-discovery and spiritual fulfillment. He achieved business success while searching for the meaning of life, despite not doing it for financial reasons. His book reveals the understanding he gained about reality based on his research of science and mysticism. He is on a mission to help others transform their lives and the world by rising above the limits of themselves and opening themselves to the energy consciousness of the universe. This sounds coincidentally quite familiar. I think that he and Aaron would hit it off.

In his video, Masri says that the universe is composed mostly of pure energy. If the space between atoms was removed, the entire mass of humanity on earth would amount to the size of a cube of sugar. The world only appears and feels solid because our brains are programmed to perceive and sense it that way. But, the energy of the universe has no boundaries, it is interconnected everywhere. He says that the energy we put out into the universe will attract and unite with similar energy. Now, I'm freaking out. This is precisely what Aaron told me!

Masri says that even the energy of fighting for causes like injustice, which we perceive as good, actually transmits the energy of fighting, anger, hatred, and negativity. This seeds the universe with negative, contracted energy. This ultimately doesn't result in improvement for the world. It

---

[9] "Limitless Manifestations Keys", Ziad Masri, FaceBook
[10] "Reality Unveiled: The Hidden Keys of Existence That Will Transform Your Life (and The World)", by Ziad Masri, 2017, Awakened Media LLP

does just the opposite. It manifests new problems from the seed of its origin. Energy of love and peace spread through the universe and affect improvement in the world.

The date on Masri's video post was November 15, 2019. Aaron's birthday. Again, wow!

Sunday February 9, 2020.

I ordered Masri's book and began to read it. My mouth is hanging open at every word. His book is essentially about that Aaron has been telling me. The universe is made up of entirely energy. We are all connected to it and in constant exchange with it. We are limited to what we can sense, and there is so much more that we are not able to know. We attract compatible energy. We must keep our own energy in healthy flow with the universe.

Masri says that what we are seeking is actually seeking us. Aaron told me the same thing when he said that it's crowded at the door to the other side. The departed want us to know that they are seeking to connect with us through that door as we seek to connect with them. We just need to open it.

Thursday February 13, 2020.

Masri's book has been mind-blowing so far. Aaron told me that it's good for me to read it, but I must keep in mind that human viewpoints are subjective. They are tied to human conceptualizations. Believe all that you want to if it brings you inner peace. But always remain open.

Aaron said that the concept of a purpose-driven universe is based on a human construct. He said, "It's ok to think about the universe that way, and to explore it to the full extent of human limits. In the reality of the entire universe, humans cannot conceptualize all of its facets."

Grief comes in like dark clouds

Some heavier than others

Sometimes a ray of comfort shines through

And reminds me of the joy you were

Because you lived, my dearest son Aaron

Camille Dan 2020

Friday February 14, 2020.

Anthony and I went to visit Aaron's grave today. Aaron told me to go there because it will help me to feel better. It's the coldest day of the winter so far. By the time we arrived it had warmed up considerably outside. The sun broke through the clouds. I think Aaron warmed it up for me.

I placed a heart-shaped rock on top of Aaron's headstone. I found it on the beach in Florida. It stood out from all of the shell fragments and sand. Jewish mourners have been putting stones on their loved one's graves for centuries. They're signs of remembrance.

I have collected quite a few stones that I keep for visiting Aaron. I brought this one today because it's Valentine's Day. Aaron gave me a card on every Valentine's Day. I miss that. Luckily, I saved them all. He wrote loving messages in every card he gave me. The heart-shaped stone is my Valentine gift for him.

When we left the cemetery, I had memories of my mother's funeral. I'm still upset and grieving over her. When I lost Aaron, the grief for my mother was completely overshadowed by the grief of losing Aaron. I just couldn't carry that much pain and trauma. It's almost like I forgot about her, and I feel bad about that.

Suddenly, I heard my mother's voice. She said that she understands. "I care more that my children are okay, and that they get along." She knows how a mother feels about her children.

Monday February 17, 2020.

We went to spend a couple of days at Anthony's cottage. Caleb came with us. Zach and Candice brought their dog, Pixel. Pixel is a cute little wire-haired terrier mix, white with a black mark on his back that looks just like Disney's Mickey Mouse icon. He's the smartest dog I've ever met. He has the most contemplative look in his big, brown, anthropomorphic eyes, that can be unsettling sometimes. There's more behind those eyes than any of us know.

It was a beautiful sunny day. We went on the frozen lake and played in the snow. Caleb loved riding in the sled. My heart has been heavy that Aaron wasn't with us there. He would have really enjoyed it.

I saw some misty clouds in the sky while I was thinking about how much I miss Aaron. There was a rainbow in the mist among them. I noticed the rainbow would brighten when I thought of my love for Aaron, and then it would dim as my thoughts turned to missing him. I tried this thinking pattern many times over, and the same thing happened every time. Amazing!

Saturday February 29, 2020.

It's been a while since I've written. A lot has been going on that has sent my anxiety through the roof. It's all related to dealing with my grief and the grief of my other children.

I asked Aaron about references to levels of existence that I had been reading. Do we really choose our incarnation for life lessons as our spirit moves up each level? Aaron said that this is another belief based on a human construct, like the purpose-driven universe he mentioned the other day. Choosing life lessons implies wants and needs. There is no want or need where he is. Energy goes where it goes. That is simple enough to understand. How the universe works is not possible for us to understand. He said that there is universal consciousness, but it is far more complex than our simplistic understanding of it.

Saturday March 7, 2020.

I went to the synagogue with a friend today. I told her that I feel more connected with Aaron there. Aaron and I used to go there together. The synagogue services are traditional, and all are welcome. Men and women sit in separate areas during prayer, so Aaron and I didn't sit together. But I knew he was there in the men's section. I was so proud of him to take it upon himself. So grown up. I still feel his presence there, even though I can't see him.

My friend and I both thought it was a good idea to brush up on our Hebrew and learn to pray. So, we attended a class on prayer. The class was cut short when the teacher said that our Rabbi wants everyone to hear his sermon. We moved over to the sanctuary. I wasn't too happy about that. I had been looking forward to the class.

The Rabbi spoke about Moses and his older brother Aaron. He said that today's parsha was all about Aaron. A parsha is the portion of the Torah that is addressed and prayed over each week on the Sabbath Day. This week's is the only parsha totally dedicated to Aaron.

He is an important figure in Judaism. He was the first High Priest of the Israelites. The Rabbi said that Aaron was devoted to his mother.

I believe that I was there to receive a message from my Aaron. He wants me to keep going there for comfort and to keep our connection intact. My friend said that she thought it was definitely a sign. I didn't mind missing the class for this!

Sunday March 8, 2020.

This morning I'm feeling very depressed. I noticed that depression is overtaking the shock. I can't seem to pull myself out of it. I was upstairs thinking about how life isn't worth living without Aaron. Maybe I'll catch Covid-19 and it'll all be over. I heard Aaron's voice say, "Mom, I'm ok where I am. Your other children need you."

Wednesday March 11, 2020.

Upon waking up this morning, I had a dreadful thought, *"I'll never see Aaron or my mother again."* All at once, I heard both of them say loud and clear, "Yes you will."

Chaos. Everything feels that way as soon as I open my eyes. Life is so random. I can't make sense of things that used to make sense. This out-of-order loss has me completely messed up. Anxiety is constantly gnawing at my gut. No amount of sleep cures my exhaustion. I give up. I need medication. I'm calling my doctor.

Aaron tells me not to think of chaos as a problem. "Chaos is necessary, Mom. Don't worry about it. Sometimes things might appear to be out of order, but they never are. Flow is order, and chaos is part of it."

My doctor prescribed me an anti-anxiety/antidepressant. I'm going to start taking it. I need something to take the edge off. Nothing else is helping enough.

Counseling helps. Writing helps. Meditation helps. Connecting with Aaron definitely helps. But the grief is too powerful, and it always takes over. Alcohol makes me sick. Sleeping pills make me sleepy all day. I'm going to follow my doctor's recommendation and take a prescription to help me get through.

Different Love

I've had to learn to love different

Not always by choice

Over a lifetime love can change

It grows and shrinks

It waxes and wanes

It shifts and curves

It swells and collapses

Love can carry you to the moon

It can bring you to your knees

But the one different love

That I can't seem to grasp

Is the love for my child who's passed

Love that has turned to pain

Only one thing can ease

Is to be with my child again.

Camille Dan 2020

Thursday March 12, 2020.

The speed of light. I asked Aaron if he can travel faster than the speed of light. He told me that energy can. He said that energy can take different forms that can travel at any speed through any time.

He explained, "Energy transfers across an infinite universe made up of infinite universes." I asked him if he can travel through time, in that case. He answered, "My energy can travel through time. But it's not forward and backward. I can't explain time to you. I can come across myself in the past. I can feel the thoughts and feelings I had." I asked him that if this is the case, can my future energy be looking at me now? He said that it can, but I have no way of knowing it because I lack the capacity to be aware of it. I hope the future me is okay with the present me.

Thursday March 26, 2020.

COVID-19 pandemic. I've been self isolating for two weeks because of my lung condition. It's called Bronchiectasis. That's a long name for chronic scarring of the lungs. This makes me more prone to lung infections because bacteria can get stuck in the scar tissue. My lung specialist said that she thinks it resulted from a serious case of pneumonia I had when I was eighteen.

Being stuck at home while grieving has its challenges. I'm distracting myself by doing major house cleaning interspersed with reading, binge-watching TV, and playing video games. I'm socializing on the phone, FB, IG, and FaceTime. I do video workouts and go for long walks in my neighbourhood with Maisie. I talk to the kids nearly every day. I call my father all the time and talk with him when he's able to pick up the phone. I think of Aaron every minute. Distracting myself helps keep the pain at bay.

I just want Aaron to come back. Sometimes, I beg him to come back. Yesterday he told me that he can't return as himself, the Aaron I knew. "Even if I do come back, I will be in another body with another brain and personality."

Aaron said that his energy flows around me and through me. He can communicate with me because I continue to communicate with him. Our energy is connected. We perceive ourselves as separate beings, but we are not.

COVID-19 is a perfect example of how we are connected by things we cannot see. Isn't it something that an invisible little bugger can change our lives so dramatically and practically overnight? We have microscopes that can see the coronavirus. We can see that it enters peoples bodies and makes them sick. But even a virus transfers energy with a cell as it replicates. Energy can't be directly seen even through a microscope. The most we can see is the result of it. So, we are more connected to each other, and to all of the energy around us than we realize.

Saturday March 28, 2020.

Automatic Writing. Also called spirit writing, or psychographic experience. Arlene had one with a message from Aaron. Someone in my online child-loss support group said that she wrote psychographic messages from her departed son. I commented to her that I found this fascinating, and I would try it. I decided to try it today. I sat with a pen in my hand and paper on my desk. I put the pen to a spot on the paper. I thought about Aaron and counted backwards until I fell into a mild trance. The pen began to move. I wasn't sure if it because of random nerve driven arm movements. But I soon realized that the top of the pen was tilting by itself and pulling my hand in different directions. I gave into it and let the ink end follow. I got tired quickly, and my curiosity lifted me out of the trance. When I looked at the paper, I was shocked with what I saw. I had written, "to CMD. Aaron." CMD are my initials. The words were written in a circular pattern, so I had to read them in a circle to see them.

Last night, Aaron told me that there is more to time and space in the universe than humans are able to measure. Time does not follow only our laws and scales, neither does space. Aaron said, "Space can be bent, kind of, and so can time. Time travel is possible. Energy has infinite potential through space and time."

Tuesday March 31, 2020.

More Covid-19. I asked Aaron, "Why is there a pandemic now?" He said that there is no such thing as "why". There's only, "is". "Things are because they are. They happen because they occur in balance with the universe.

The universe is never out of balance, or rebalancing. Universal energy is always balanced. How this pandemic is happening can be explained. But the explanation involves an infinite amount of data."

Wednesday April 1, 2020.

I didn't want to wake up this morning because Aaron was in my dream last night. I wanted to stay asleep where I was with him. The dream was so vivid. I heard his voice. He called my cell phone. I knew it was him. He said that he was in Israel. Then, he was here at home with me. I felt his hug. It felt so real. I could feel our love for each other. I just want to go back to sleep and see him again. But he's not in my dreams every night.

I can't stop crying this morning. The pain of missing Aaron is too much. It's heavier than any weight imaginable. I have never experienced pain worse than this.

Friday April 10, 2020.

Still Covid-19. We are sheltering in place. More and more the government is enforcing social distancing. They have imposed a stiff fine of $1,000 for anyone caught in violation of the one-meter-apart rule. Grocery stores are limiting the amount of food and supplies we are each allowed. The furthest I go beyond my house is for a walk around the block.

The house is cleaner than it has been in years. I'm cleaning everything to the nooks and crannies. I heard Aaron calling my name repeatedly again today. I tried asking him what it's about. No answer.

Saturday April 11, 2020.

Today, I heard Aaron calling my name again. He still hasn't answered me why he's doing this. Now I'm worried.

Monday April 13, 2020.

While cleaning out cupboards and shelves, I found an old journal I had misplaced. It's a journal I kept when the kids were young. I wrote down things they said. I started it when I realized that Aaron was talking way before I expected him to. He was quite precocious.

I was afraid I would break down crying. I read it anyway and ended up in a pool of tears. The first page is the title page, "A Special Book About My Son, Aaron Reuben Dan. Date: February 21, 1990". In it, I recorded that Aaron began to talk at around 10 months of age.

By 15 months of age, Aaron spoke in full sentences. One night at 2 years of age, as he looked out the window, he began to sing "Twinkle Little Star" and added a few verses of his own. "The moon is in the sky...The world is in the sky...The stars are in the sky...But I can't touch the stars...And I can't touch the moon...I wish I could touch the stars."

Wednesday April 15, 2020.

Aaron's grandfather sent me a question. "Can you contact Aaron and ask him if he can tell you how soon the coronavirus will be over, and life will become normal. Entities existing in the "parallel world" frequently seem to have universal knowledge. Perhaps Aaron can respond."

Aaron answered. He said that the Covid-19 pandemic will be over in 5 months, and then there will be places where it will spring up again. This will temporarily interfere with some travel and business, but it won't recur as a pandemic again. He said that a vaccine will start to be given around October or November 2020. He said that it will take about a decade for people to live without it on their minds.

Friday April 17, 2020.

Aaron told me this morning that he feels more helpful than ever. He said he will watch over Jonathan at work. Jonathan is the only person I know who got a job during the pandemic. He takes fastidious steps to prevent spreading Covid-19. I'm worried for him, but not worried too. He's very careful, and he has Aaron watching over him.

Aaron said something very interesting last night. He told me, "I am with Omi and Mimi who are helping me to be helpful. You're here too, Mom, and so is everyone else. There's really nothing dividing our energy exchange. You're just not able to see it past your 3-dimensional limits."

Saturday April 18, 2020.

Leslie sent this question, "I have been very close to my daughter, and she is close to me too. I have a very interesting question to Aaron. "Have my daughter and my self – Papa – being together in our previous lives, perhaps more often and we have now re-incarnated." I wonder if Aaron can respond."

This was Aaron's answer, "Hi Papa, Mom asked me your question, and it's a very complicated one. People can't see the extent of how energy behaves in the universe. Transfer of energy is beyond human measures. But yes, you and your daughter have been together in the same way you and I have been together across time and incarnations."

Wednesday April 22, 2020.

Aaron said that energy is unencumbered where he is. "While we are embodied, we can have physical and mental conditions and illnesses that cause us to appear to be ourselves. But the essence of who we really are might be very different. Disease can be an obstacle to connection with compatible energy. After life, those conditions are left behind with the body." Where Aaron is there is no illness or limitation.

Tuesday April 28, 2020.

Numerology. I'm not good at math. I don't know anything about numerology. It's apparently a belief system based on the relationship between numbers and events. It's kind of like astrology, except with numbers instead of zodiac signs.

A few days ago, Aaron pointed out something about numbers to me. His birthdate, 15-11, and Zach's birthdate, 15-11, correspond to the Hebrew name for God, יהוה.
יYad=10, הHeh=5, וVav=6, הHeh=5. Or 10+5=15, 6+5=11. Or, 15+11. That totals 26.

Each letter of the Hebrew alef-bet (alphabet) has a corresponding number. The relationship between letters and numbers in Hebrew is called, Gematria. Words have numerical values when their letters are added together. The basis of Kabbalistic belief is in the Gematria. Practitioners of Kabbalah rely on this type of numerology for their mystical interpretations of the Torah. Their belief is that the Torah is the blueprint for the creation of God's perfect universe.

From the little that I've recently read about this practice, I can see that the depth of study involved in Kabbalah is beyond me and my lifetime. But I'm thinking a beginner course would be interesting.

This numerology thing has been revolving around in my mind since Aaron mentioned it. I asked him what it means.

He told me that I'll never understand it all until I'm where he is. "The meaning of this is beyond the understanding of great mathematical minds, Mom. No offense, but I can never get you to understand it."

Today, Aaron added more detail. He told me that my birthdate, 26-07, adds up to 15, and his father's birthdate adds up to 11. Again, 15 and 11. I asked him that since 15 plus 11 equal 26, is there any significance to that?

Aaron told me that there is a lot of significance in it. He said that it is extremely rare for events to occur like this coincidentally. When this does happen, it indicates something. He told me to try adding together our family's Hebrew birthdates. So, I did.

Together they total 26. Aaron and Zach's Hebrew birthdates add up to 15, and their father's and my Hebrew birthdates add up to 11. 15 plus 11 equal 26.

Also, Aaron's grandparent's birth dates contain these same numbers. My mother's, 11-11 or 11-14, my father's, 11-18, Aaron's other grandmother, 3-23 (total 26), and his other grandfather, 11-26.

Ok. What does this all mean? Aaron has been giving me information in bits and pieces here and there. I never know if there will be more coming. It's up to me to figure it all out. Today he told me that he needs to be where he is. I hope he will tell me more in days to come.

Wednesday April 29, 2020.

Aaron told me this morning that numbers together represent intersections. He said that there are more indicators that we can perceive that he will try to explain. He said that the numbers point ways to how we can know

121

that our dimensions are connected. He said that there are significant events associated with the numbers. He said that his grandfather's numbers, 26-11, are associated with two tablets and Ten Commandments. He said that nothing is simple, and everything is interconnected on many levels. He said that things that occur simultaneously can seem to be separated by time. But they aren't necessarily.

This evening, I received an email confirming that $11,564.00 of the Aaron Dan Memorial Fund will be directed to an organization in which he participated and helped. I believe that Aaron would want to give this donation. The remainder is to go to urgent needs during the pandemic, which I believe Aaron would also have given to. He was so willing to drop anything to help someone in need.

Just saying that the amount going to charity adds up to 26. $11+(5+6+4) =11+15=26. The numbers add up. They are telling me something. I think they're indicating that Aaron and I are on this journey together. I'll follow the numbers.

Monday May 4, 2020.

Aaron told me today that love is eternal. Energy has no feelings, but feelings are energy. Feelings arise from biological sources, and they also affect biological events. Transfer and exchange of energy is affected by feelings. Love energy is always compatible with flow.

May 5, 2020. How Could You Leave?

It was so sudden. There was no sign, no premonition. You were too young. Life was just beginning. A new chapter was opening. You had everything going for you. Intelligence,

kindness, generosity, wit, capability, magnetism. You were
making plans and going places. You were 31. The world was
your oyster. You were moving up. I was so proud. I was
right by your side, through thick and thin. You were
supposed to be here. I was supposed to be cheering for you
all the way, all my life. What the hell happened? How could
you leave before me, my son? How could you leave me
here? How could you leave?

Thursday May 14, 2020.

Aaron's grandfather called today to ask Aaron another question. He wanted to know if a treatment for cancer that his company is working on will be successful, and if it will get an approval next year. As soon as I hung up the phone, Aaron said he heard the question. He said, "Mom, everything Papa touches turns to gold."

Then Aaron stated, "Antibody. The treatment uses antibodies." He showed me a visual image for the first time. I could see a mental picture of an antibody attached to a molecule entering a cell causing it to explode.

I was curious if Aaron was right. When I told Leslie what Aaron said, he was shocked. Sure enough, the treatment uses antibodies that attach to and kill the cancer cells. Aaron was exactly right. He said that the treatment will be well-received and approved. He said that it has potential and will work on other cancers. Leslie asked me to say thank you to Aaron. Aaron said to tell Papa that he heard him.

Sunday May 17, 2020.

Last Sunday was Mother's Day. It was also the one-year anniversary of my mother's death. How can I ever have another happy Mother's Day? I'm sure that I won't. I tried to let it slide by unnoticed. That didn't work. It feels like my heart didn't beat for the whole week.

I think Aaron and my mother knew how bad I would feel at this time. They sent me a male and female cardinal. I captured a photo of the male.

Male Cardinal

Thursday May 21, 2020.

I keep thinking about the birth date numbers. How coincidental that three generations of birthdates all contain the same numbers that make up the name of God. Aaron told me today that God's name adds up to 26, and 2+6=8. 8 is the symbol for infinity: ∞.

Aaron said that not only do the letters of the name of God in Hebrew add up to 26, God in English, G (letter no. 7), O (letter no. 15), D (letter no. 4), 7+15+4, also adds up to 26.

He hasn't given more information about the common numbers in the family birth dates. But he said that there has been a powerful energy present within our family. We have revolved around each other in eternity. He said that he knows infinity is difficult to imagine.

Monday May 25, 2020.

For the past couple of months, doors in the house have been closing on their own. They have never done this before. It's not always the same door. Yesterday, after a shower I found my bedroom door half closed. It was fully open when I went in there before my shower. No one was home. Oddly, I wasn't scared.

I touched the door and said, "Aaron?" In that instant a very cold breeze blew along the hand and arm that I had on the door. I looked around. There is no air vent even near that door. Then, I heard Aaron say, "Yes mom, I'm here."

After that, when I was downstairs in the kitchen, one of the French doors began to slowly close itself as I watched it. My closet door now closes itself when I'm in there. All of the doors usually stay open. There's no apparent reason for doors to sometimes close by themselves. I really hope it's Aaron giving me signs.

Wednesday May 27, 2020.

While sitting on my back porch, I looked at the sky and saw clouds in the shape of an A with a heart above it on the left. I was lucky to get a photo. Aaron said that he did it for me.

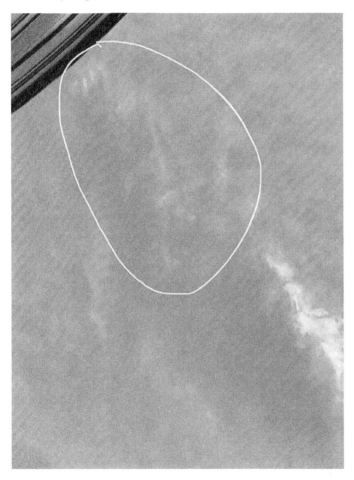

"A" With a Heart on Top

Just as I began to cry, a cardinal flew close to me. He wasn't afraid. He let me take a photo of him.

Lingering Cardinal

Saturday May 30, 2020.

Lights are going off and on by themselves. The TV changed channels on its own tonight. Aaron is trying to get my attention. I wonder why. Maybe to reassure me that he's still here by sending me these signs.

Friday June 5, 2020.

For the last couple of days, Aaron has been telling me that humans are the highest manifestation of energy and matter in our dimension. Humans have the highest abilities because of this. Today, he explained, "To a rock, humans would appear to have unlimited abilities. To humans, spirits are thought to have unlimited abilities."

"This all has to do with how energy and matter work together", he said, "Energy is infinite, matter is finite. Energy moves through space (which is itself) and time (which is energy influencing itself) at varying speeds of space-time. Free energy moves very fast, while the energy that forms a rock, in contrast, moves very slow. The energy within humans is moving somewhere in between."

He added, "The exchange of energy between particles, molecules and matter is imperceptible. Time behaves differently depending on the state that the energy is in. Energy can jump between states to any dimension. This can also occur simultaneously because of its influence on time. Energy in the form of free conscience moves too fast for detection in the human dimension, but here it has freedom to flow and be."

Colours of After

Blue is the grief that washes over me

Like waves of the ocean

The depth of the sea

Red is the cardinal who comes to visit me

He tells me you are near

Through his eyes you do see

Yellow is the sun shining on me

Warming relief

Of your radiant energy

White are the clouds so soft and carefree

Forming shapes and your name

In Calligraphy

Green is the colour of my backyard tree

Shading the guilt

That it should have been me

Orange is the flame of memory

Forever in keeping

Under lock and key

Violet is the color of reverie

Counting on dreams

Of what was and will be

Gray is the shade of mystery

The pain and the longing

An eternity

Clear is the colour of clarity

That one day again son

It will be you and me

Camille Dan 2020

Sunday June 7, 2020.

Today was my first day in the pool this year. Aaron loved the summer, and we had many good times in the backyard chatting, barbecuing, and swimming. I love to swim, especially on the hot, sunny days. I was really sad without Aaron there. I looked up to the sky and saw that the clouds spelled Aaron very clearly. In cursive! I love his cloud signs.

I couldn't get out of the pool and to my phone fast enough to get a photo this time. By the time I got to my phone, and scrambled to find the camera app, the cloud formation had changed. It goes to show how instantaneous the signs are. What are the odds of being in exactly the right spot, at the most advantageous angle, at the precise moment to see them? Extremely small, I would think. Probably incalculable.

At the same time, a beautiful butterfly hovered over me watching me fumble and curse at my phone. That's a lot of signs at once!

Monday June 8, 2020.

On Sunday, Jonathan visited. We talked about how we're both having such a hard time without Aaron. Jonathan told me how angry he is. He has been looking for blame. I told Jonathan that everyone was to blame in some way for what happened to Aaron. Everyone played their part. But no one had bad intentions. Parents make mistakes, but they love their children. I told him that I apologize for my mistakes, but I always love and value my children.

Aaron told me today why he suffered from emotional issues growing up. He said that he grew up thinking that he could always trust his parents. He said that he lost trust at too young an age to understand. When he got older, Aaron said that he didn't believe he could trust anyone. He said that this tore him up inside. He told me that he did come to learn to trust, which gave him more confidence and value in himself. He said that he wanted me to know that to help me to feel better. I did want to know that he valued himself as I so valued him.

Friday June 12, 2020.

Today, Aaron told me that my Out-of-Body-Experience happened during my pregnancy with him so that I would know that he was meant to live, and that we will always be, and have always been together. While out of my body I learned about universal consciousness and connectedness. I returned to my body so that Aaron would be born and live.

Thursday June 18, 2020.

I spoke to Arlene today. I told her that, out of the blue, her mother told me to say Hi to her. Arlene told me that she's been stressed and needs support. Now we know why her mother told me to contact her.

Monday June 22, 2020.

Aaron sent me a heart of clouds today.

Heart in the Clouds

Tuesday June 30, 2020.

Aaron has been talking to me on the subject of Black Holes lately. He said that they are a good example of something that exists beyond our senses. Aaron said, "You know Black Holes exist because you can see indications of some of them. But, since you can't see inside of them, you have to guess at what might be by analogy.

If one- and two-dimensional objects had senses, they would still lack the ability to see the entirety of three-dimensional things. Humans and three-dimensional objects lack the ability to sense anything that exists beyond three dimensions. But they might be able to sense that part of something beyond three dimensions that intersects with their world."

"What I mean is, a one-dimensional line lacks width and height. So, it would perceive (if it had senses) a person to be just a point along a line, but nothing more. It can't see that the person also has two more dimensions. A two-dimensional object has height and width, but it lacks depth. So, it would perceive a person without thickness, and it can't see the rest of the person beyond its own scope."

Aaron said that Black Holes balance energy and intersect dimensions. All we can see is the point of intersection. But there is much more beyond that. "Energy exists in different forms. Black Holes arise as part of balancing things. You could say that they are dimensions in of themselves. They are energy flowing at rates that are imperceptible by other forms of matter. They can be any size, massive, or microscopic. There might be one right beside you, but you won't know it. Because human existence is a product of matter, we are built to perceive things as objects that occupy space. The universe is more than that, and dimensions exist beyond just three," he said.

The dimension of time is difficult for us to perceive in its entirety, other than how it operates in the three-dimensional space. It is not just linear. Aaron said "Physicists can only theorize about time within the scope of their ability to observe and measure it. Energy is free to flow beyond the three-dimensional world. There are dimensions all around you, just beyond your senses. What occurs in dimensions beyond yours affects what happens in your three-dimensions, and vice versa."

Aaron went further to say, "This could be thought of as pre-determination, and where the concept of a Creator comes from. Consider that forces from other dimensions are causing what's happening in the human world. Or, that things that are happening in the human world are flowing toward forces in other dimensions."

I hope there won't be a test on this, but Aaron is convincing me that much more exists beyond what I can see.

Friday July 3, 2020.

Because of Covid-19, it was quiet at the hospital when I went for my routine CT scan today. There were only a couple of other people in the waiting room, masked and socially distancing six feet apart (sorry, two metres apart if you're in Canada). It was so quiet that I could hear Aaron very clearly. He told me that he was there with me. I asked him if he knows when and how someone will die. He said that it's not good for balance to know.

Wednesday July 8, 2020.

Today, Aaron talked about mitochondria. These are the tiny organelles present in our cells that convert food energy into energy that our cells can use for their functions. Mitochondria possess their own unique DNA, which suggests that they did not originate from within human cells. They resemble bacteria in structure. At some time, they became symbiotic with human cells. But before that, they existed on their own. They had their own DNA and manufactured their own energy.

The Mitochondrial Eve theory says that all modern humans arose from a single mother because we all possess the same mitochondrial DNA. MtDNA is passed through the mother to all male and female offspring. This is how connected our cells and mitochondria have become. Our cells exist in an energy exchange with them.

Aaron told me, "The symbiosis with mitochondria is a microcosm of the universe, as is everything. To mitochondria, each person is a universe. Yet, there is so much more beyond each one. We are connected with the universe in a similar way. We live within our perceived universe, which is really part of the much bigger one."

"People are so firmly rooted in a three-dimensional reality, believing things to be separate entities. They think, I am separate from you. I am separate from a tree, my car, etc., etc. But we aren't separate at all, not even from our cars. We enter a system of energy exchange with our car from the purchase through its use. We are not separate from that system. Nothing in the universe is separate from anything else", he said.

Tuesday July 14, 2020.

Aaron told me that we really are together in eternity with everyone. While in our human form, we are only aware of the relationships that we can observe. He said, "I am aware of all interactions. Exchanges I had while in human form can be re-experienced here." Aaron said that we should try to make our relationships as loving as possible while we are on earth because we will ultimately all be together in eternity. "We create our eternal experience, Mom."

Tuesday July 21, 2020.

The stabbing pain of the upcoming tenth monthiversary of Aaron's passing has been crippling. Today, he told me that love is a very complicated energy for people. "Love doesn't always feel good, Mom. Sometimes it can feel very painful, confusing, and unhealthy. Love is energy that is always present. It is part of everything. When love is unhealthy, or confusing, it's energy cycling. It takes very powerful energy to break unhealthy cycles. But eventually it will come, and its energy will flow back to the universe."

Wednesday July 22, 2020.

Today I have reached ten months of grieving. I woke up this morning from a beautiful dream of Aaron and I on a road trip. We detoured from one quaint little town to another. Our interests were captured by the beautiful scenery, welcoming townsfolk, country style shops and restaurants. It was such a pleasant dream of spending time together. It felt so real. When I woke up, I felt let down. We never got to where we were going. Metaphorical, for sure.

This evening, Arlene and I went to a friend's backyard for a socially distant visit. The Covid-19 rate has been declining for the past couple of months. We are permitted to meet, only in small groups while keeping six feet or two meters apart.

I'm still nervous about socializing during the pandemic, so I wore a mask. I only took it off for the occasional sip from my glass of rosé. Underneath my Covid protection mask is my other mask. I put it on first before visiting anyone. My mask looks like me with a fake smile that hides my grief.

Our friend has an adorable new puppy. I brought Maisie to play. We began a conversation about afterlife, and I told my friend some of what I hear from Aaron. I used the word "leap" in a sentence. At exactly that moment, the puppy leaped into my lap. We looked at each other aghast and laughed. Evident synchronicity.

Thursday July 23, 2020.

Today, I joined a Zoom video Parsha class with my rabbi. When he spoke about Adam and Eve, and Good and Evil, Aaron clarified the story for me. He is an intellectual and a historian. He loves to discuss the significance of biblical stories.

Aaron commented, "The story of Adam and Eve represents the dawn of man and connection to universal energy. Because human brains have superior analytical ability, choices can be made by higher analysis and instinct, unlike other earthly creatures that only act on instinct. Follow the dots. Adam arose from the soil. Eve came from Adam. So, we are not entirely separate beings from each other, or from earthly matter. Adam and Eve shared and exchanged conscious energy. They communicated and learned from each other. Humans regard choice as decision between good and evil, or pros vs. cons, since these concepts can be readily quantified to their dimension. Adam and Eve were not banished from the Garden of Eden. When they chose to enter earthly manifestations, their spirit energy infused their bodies. In their earthly existence, they became unable to perceive of their spirit existence in the dimensions beyond themselves."

July 24, 2020. The Story in the Story

Man plans and God laughs is how the saying goes, I think. What did God do with all of the plans I had with my son? ROFL?

We were only halfway through our story. It wasn't supposed to go the way it did. We didn't even consider this. Everything was supposed to go as planned, or at least close enough to it. Anything unexpected, or unpleasant arose, we could handle it. If a pleasant unexpected something arose, it was a welcome gift.

We had it all worked out. A balanced life was our way to live our story the way we planned it. How were we to know that some event on the other side of the universe would interrupt our balance?

Our story collided with the universe. We didn't know that the path we were on would lead to here. How could we know? We couldn't.

Now what? Everything feels off balance without my son. I'm totally off balance. I try to re-balance, but that doesn't happen. What is balance, anyway? When I felt balanced, I wasn't. It wasn't real.

Maybe I'll find a new balance, maybe I won't. I don't know where to look for it. I'll just go with how I feel from one moment to the next and leave balance up to the universe.

Sunday July 26, 2020.

My first birthday without Aaron. Enough said.

Friday July 31, 2020.

Aaron reminds me often that we're still together. I told him that this is comforting. But I'd prefer it if we were together in 3D. He told me to not dwell too much on incarnations. He said, "We are with each other all of the time, as we are incarnated with the eternal energy of the universe."

Thursday August 6, 2020.

Aaron told me today that I already know that consciousness can be projected out of the body. It happened to me during my out-of-body-experience. He said, "Mom, you already know that consciousness doesn't need a body to exist. You've been there yourself. You don't have to question it."

I know it, but grief is a confusing roller coaster ride. No matter what you thought you knew, it all slipped away. You're trying to hold on to something elusive.

Sunday August 9, 2020.

Aaron told me that he will be there for me at my time to cross over. I asked him to be. I think about seeing him again one day. Some days, I feel like I can't wait for it. Aaron said, "We will know each other instantly. We have been connected in eternity. Our connection remains because of our eternal love for each other."

I asked him if everyone has the same kind of experience when they cross over. He said, "Everyone's experience is different depending on the strength of love they have, and on the depth of their wisdom. The more love, the more readily the transition will be. The deeper the wisdom, the clearer the crossing. By wisdom, I'm not talking about intelligence. An infant can be wiser than an adult. It can happen that some people have a more confusing transition. But that's very rare."

Tuesday August 11, 2020.

Love is wisdom. Aaron told me that he wants me to try to stay in a more positive mindset. It will help us to remain connected. He told me that dwelling on negativity, anxiety, worries, depression, anger, and other unhealthy energy will result in distancing and separation of our energies. He told me to try to keep our energy compatible, strong and flowing together.

On today's news there was a headline that Russia will begin inoculating the public with a vaccine against Covid-19 around the end of October or beginning of November this year. Aaron was right about when a vaccine will be given. I consider this prediction to be evidence that he spoke to me.

Wednesday August 12, 2020.

Doors are opening by themselves again. The utility room door slowly opened by itself in front of my eyes. I called out to Aaron, and an icy cold draft crossed my shoulder. There is no vent there, either. So, it wasn't the air conditioner kicking on. It was Aaron.

I told Aaron that I miss him so much. My heart is still broken. Not a moment goes by that I don't think of him. He told me that he knows. He can't explain his accident to me, but he wasn't ready to die. He has decided to come back. He said that I will know him when I see him. He can't tell me when this will happen yet.

Saturday August 15, 2020.

I went to Arlene's house for coffee today. We sat on her roof top patio. We spoke a lot about energy and afterlife. She told me Aaron had visited her recently to say he'll be with me tomorrow at his unveiling. The cover will be removed from his headstone. The thought of reading my son's headstone is gut-wrenching.

Suddenly, a "disturbance in the ether" appeared alongside Arlene. An Aaron-shaped blur hung in the atmosphere. I thought it might be some kind of weird mirage. Or, at my age, maybe my eyesight is going. I shifted my eyes and blinked a few times. But it remained fixed in place.

It stayed there for most of our conversation. I really hope it was Aaron. I'm so upset about tomorrow, and that he's not here to give me one of his hugs. I miss him more and more.

Sunday August 16, 2020.

Aaron's unveiling. The dreaded day has arrived to uncover the headstone. Zachary and Candice came. Jonathan came too. Anthony was there. Shelby's friend came with her for support. I've always liked her. Papa and Anna attended. Rabbi Elie was there when we arrived. Extended family came. Everyone wore a mask because of Covid-19. We all stood ceremoniously six feet apart around Aaron's grave. It felt surreal.

The rabbi prayed with us and delivered a beautiful speech, as did Jonathan and Leslie. They all spoke to Aaron as if he was present there. I think he was. Leslie's speech was touching and loving. Jonathan spoke about missing his big brother, and what a positive influence he was. I spoke briefly and shakily, thanking everyone for the love they showed Aaron throughout his life.

Tuesday August 18, 2020.

There was an "A" in the clouds today, and wow! I got a good, clear photo of it.

"A" Written In Clouds

Thursday August 20, 2020.

Today was a beautiful day. Cindy and I had coffee on my
back porch. I showed her the photo of the "A" that I saw
written in a cloud on Tuesday. She said she wished for
things like that from her father.

No kidding, right above her head there were her father's
initials, "ZF", written in clouds! I wish you could have seen
the expression on her face. She looked surprised, happy,
reassured, and grateful all at once. Luckily, I had my phone
with me, and I got a good photo of Cindy's wow moment.

"ZF" Written In Clouds

A Blessing in Grief

May friendship be your lighthouse

In this broken-heart darkness

May companionship rescue you

When you crash against rocks

As you drift on this sea of grief

May understanding warm you

From the chill of despair

May empathy comfort you

When the anguish feels unfathomable

And there is no horizon in sight

May support be ever present

Through this uncharted journey you're on

May the weight of your pain be buoyed

By the angels around you

And the kindness of others

May you be eternally blessed

Camille Dan 2020

Friday August 21, 2020.

Finally, I am buying a cottage. I've wanted one for as long as I can remember. But, because of family and extended family obligations, I haven't given myself the right to buy extras for myself. Plus, with the emotional weight those obligations, I didn't think I could handle another responsibility. Things have changed.

Today I looked at cottage listings. Nothing seemed exactly right, but there were a couple of places that might do. Anthony and I drove to cottage country to have a look around. Neither place was overly appealing. In fact, one of them was a tear-down, a hard no. But the other one had possibilities. I decided to go home and think it over.

On our way home, my real estate agent called to say that another cottage just came on the market today. We could turn around if we wanted to look at it. We hadn't yet gone far, so we said yes.

The first thing I noticed as we pulled up to the cottage was that it had the "Cape Cod" look that I hoped for. I entered the front door, and it was love at first sight. It was just what I was looking for. Brand new, bright, and cozy. The whole lakefront was windows.

I imagined myself gazing at that breathtaking view in tranquil comfort. It felt right. That's when I heard Aaron say, "I really like it, Mom." Everything seemed to have fallen into place. I turned to my agent and said, "Sold."

On the way home, Aaron's absence washed over me like a rogue wave. As much as I love the new place as a refuge for our family, he won't be there to enjoy it with us. He will never have been there. Then, I heard him say, "I will be there, Mom. I'm always with you."

Thursday September 3, 2020.

After wanting a cottage for pretty much my whole life, the stars aligned. I closed the purchase today. I wish Aaron was here to celebrate our new cottage. It's a beautiful little place that faces west, so we get all of the spectacular sunsets. The sky turns a fiery orange, and the lake glimmers with gold, as the sun kisses us goodnight on the horizon. There's a beach on one side, and a boat dock on the other. The lake side has a big deck, and a fire pit. On clear nights, the sky is a blanket of stars. The moon's glow reflects and dances on the lake. The property is surrounded by trees. There are a few small islands in view in the lake. Nearby, there's a marina. The lake is surrounded by forests full of hiking trails and wildlife.

The only thing the cottage doesn't have is Aaron. But the kids and I love it. I hope it will be our place to gather together and relax for years to come. I will spend a lot of time there perfecting my ability to communicate with Aaron. It's the ideal place to practice inner balance and peace.

Friday September 4, 2020.

This is Labour Day weekend, and the kids want to spend it at the cottage. I just got the keys yesterday. Impossible. There isn't a stick of furniture in the whole place. But, as crazy as it sounds, I had a feeling that I could make it livable within a couple of days. I was as excited as the kids.

Somehow, everything kept falling into place. I was able to buy all the furniture we needed on sale, and have it delivered the next day. Anthony and I shopped discount stores like fiends from morning to night, until we couldn't stand up anymore. We nearly bought out the whole town.

147

We were on a first-name basis with all the shopkeepers in no time. We moved in that Saturday. Unheard of. Superhuman speed. Aaron must have been there clearing the way.

Tuesday September 8, 2020.

Heading back to Toronto from the cottage, I realized that it's almost a year since we lost Aaron. A minute and an eternity ago. I was driving. So, I was trying not to relive it all in my mind while behind the wheel. Down the road from our cottage, we passed a sign that said, "Arlene's Answer". I think Aaron was trying to tell me not to dwell on the incident of his death. He was reminding me about what he said to Arlene right after it happened.

When I got home, I threw a load of laundry from the cottage in the washing machine. There's a lot of mundane things to do upon returning home. Focussing on tasks can provide a distraction from grief. There was a dime sitting in the bottom of the washer when I pulled out all the clothes. Another sign of the dimes!

Saturday September 12, 2020.

We came back up to the cottage again, already. We love it, and there's still a lot of work needing to be done to get settled in. I'd like to have some additions put on, like a bigger deck and a little bunkie by the water. All in good time.

In the evening, while relaxing inside after a tiring day's work, one of the sliding screen doors began to open and shut by itself. It was a windy day, so I thought it was the wind at first. But can the wind blow a door in two opposite

148

directions? How was the door both opening and closing on its own? Everything else was being blown in only one direction. I took a video of it.

Aaron said, "The wind is helping me, but I'm strong enough to do it. Mimi and I are here, and she's helping." The kids called my mother "Mimi". It's French slang for "Grandma". They are both here with us.

Tuesday September 22, 2020.

Damn, I woke up. I'm still waking up every day to this never-ending grief. Sleep is my only chance for a break from it. Most mornings, I wish that I hadn't woken up. But today is special. It's the first anniversary of Aaron's passing.

Some people call this day his "Angelversary". I guess that makes it seem more palatable. I still hate the sound of the "D" word. I would have slept through today if I could have.

I wouldn't mind sleeping through life. I'm not suicidal, but sometimes the thought of never waking up again feels like it would put a final end to this grief.

Saturday September 26, 2020.

We bought a couple of kayaks yesterday. They're bright orange. We got life jackets for ourselves and the dogs. The dogs jump excitedly into the kayaks. They're always thrilled to go with us, until they realize they're on a ride to the middle of a lake. Then, they jump out of the kayaks into the water. They do the same thing every time like it's never happened before. That's why we love them...and why they need life jackets. Dogs are nature's comedians.

Today, we went on a tour of the lake in our kayaks. It was fun, and a great work out, with beautiful scenery. Afterwards, as I was walking outside the cottage by the kitchen windows, I saw a shadowy figure standing inside. It looked a lot like Aaron. Everyone was outside. I believe it was him.

Sunday September 27, 2020.

Driving back to Toronto, I was able to connect with Aaron. I asked him what his experience of passing was like. He told me, "At first I didn't know what was happening. It was very dark. I looked down at my body, and it looked a bit mangled."

I asked him if he suffered any pain. He said that the pain was momentary and instantly forgotten. "In all of that darkness, a spinning circle of light appeared. I went toward it because there was nothing else but emptiness. As I approached the light circle, it felt like I was being absorbed into it. I felt Mimi's energy was part of it."

I asked him if his other grandmother, Omi, was there. Aaron said that he didn't recognize anyone else's energy there. He said that Omi's energy was not concentrated in that light circle as much as Mimi's was. But he knew Omi's energy was readily accessible if he needed it.

Friday October 23, 2020.

With so much of my attention on the new cottage, I feel like I hear from Aaron a bit less. He tells me that he's always around and I can connect with him any time. This week, with the US presidential election looming, I've been asking him if he can tell me what will happen.

It's a contentious race between Joe Biden and Donald Trump. It's been a terrible year with this pandemic, and the US has been hard hit by it. Tensions are very high. There have been protests across the country that have turned violent. The nation is divided along many lines, including racial, political, and economic. People are even divided over wearing a mask. I can't believe that there could be anti-maskers during a pandemic. The whole world is upside down.

Aaron said that predicting the future is extremely complicated. He said that it is not something that the universe tends to do. It can be done, but not by a human person. In those cases, it's good guessing. There are so many variables. Sometimes, a prediction will seem close to, or very accurate.

Sometimes it will be totally wrong. The outcome will fall into a range. The range of possibilities can be vast, or narrow. So, if it's narrow, it's easier to guess.

Aaron said that he doesn't recommend dwelling on what might happen in the future. He said that it really won't help settle anxieties and worries. He said, "Your life is about living it, and your understanding will come when you are where I am. In life, knowing what will happen next might actually make things worse, so appreciate the moments you are in."

Then he said, "It will be close, but not comfortable, Mom. Trump won't abide by the results."

Friday October 30, 2020.

This morning, while on my video fitness training, I heard noises outside the cottage. With all of the Covid-19 restrictions, I'm doing virtual work outs with my trainer.

Maisie started barking so loud, I had to go take a look at what was making all that racket. Out the window, I saw two blue jays on my eavestrough pulling out leaves and throwing them to the ground.

I told my trainer, "there are two beautiful blue birds cleaning out my eaves troughs for me." Before I finished my sentence, I heard a different noise coming from outside. Again, I went over to the window. In the driveway was the eavestrough cleaning guy. What are the odds of this incredible timing! I immediately thought of Aaron as I do every time I see a cardinal or a blue jay. Was this a sign from him telling me that he's around?

After my workout, I went to the hardware store. I've been there every day to pick up one item or another as needed. When I returned to my car, there was a giant leaf-shaped cloud in the sky over the parking lot. I took a photo. It was a sign from Aaron telling me that he was in the blue jay who was just at the cottage cleaning the leaves, and he came with me to the store. That's a lot of synchronicity in the signs.

I got a clear photo of the leaf cloud.

Leaf Shaped Cloud

Monday November 9, 2020.

Aaron told me a bit more about energy connections today. He said that every connection we make stays forever. Our consciousness, or awareness of this isn't necessary for it to be. Our unconscious is a part of it, and it knows all the energy connections of the universe. It is not merely focussed on the three dimensions of our conscious awareness. He explained, "Our unconscious awareness knows everything. We can choose what to focus on while we are alive. We can attract certain energy this way. But we cannot create, erase, or control the energy of our unconscious. It is always connected with the universe and every energy exchange we make. Every moment is linked forward and backward through time."

Saturday November 14, 2020.

I ordered a beautiful birthday cake for Zachary, and had it sent to him today. It's the day before his birthday. I know how hard tomorrow will be for him. It's Aaron's birthday tomorrow, too.

I struggled with what to do. Zach will turn 30 tomorrow. It's his milestone birthday. I want to celebrate him. But I can't dismiss my feelings about Aaron's absence. I can't assume how Zachary will feel, either. So, I decided to celebrate the day before.

Over time, the shock of sudden and unexpected loss morphs into an unwelcome acknowledgement of its reality. The sorrow runs so deep that it permeates every aspect of life. It creeps into every corner and crevice of existence until it has infiltrated your entire being and taken substantial and interstitial residence within. You become a stranger to yourself. Everything is changed.

Zachary sent me a photo of his cake when it arrived. The moment I opened his message, the sun streamed through the window onto the table in front of me. It looked like "AARN" was carved into the table. I was lucky to get a photo of it. Once the sun ray was gone, it was gone. I tried to recreate the phenomenon by shining a flashlight onto the table. The carved name didn't reappear. I had never noticed it before, and I have never seen it since. Aaron let me know he was there for his and Zach's birthday, and to go to the cemetery where his name is also carved.

Vanishing "AARN" Carved Into Wood Table

Sunday November 15, 2020.

I've been anticipating this day for a year. Aaron and Zach's birthday. We will celebrate with a cloud of sadness. We will every year.

We went to the cemetery today to honour Aaron on his birthday and to tell him that we all love him. It still doesn't seem completely real to be standing there. It seems like you stepped into an alternate reality where things happen backwards. In the real world, you don't outlive your child. I felt a chill go down my spine as I looked at his name carved into the tombstone. It was an unusually windy and cold day. The symbolism was fitting. The energy was powerful.

The timing of his name carved into the table proved to be prophetic of this moment.

Monday November 23, 2020.

My father has been in the hospital for a few weeks now. He was admitted with aspiration pneumonia. Thankfully, he's Covid-negative. He has become very frail lately. He won't be able to go back to the assisted living home after discharge.

I helped move his things to his new room at a nursing home. It's ready for when he leaves the hospital. I hate to see him go to a nursing home, and I know he doesn't want to. He was supposed to be discharged last week, but the pneumonia came back.

My sister, Rene has been helpful from afar. She lives in New Orleans. She has organized all the necessary paperwork for my father, and coordinated many people and variables concerned. She's doing as much as possible between the US and Canada during the pandemic. It hasn't been easy on her. She cares deeply for our father and hasn't been able to visit him in months other than on the phone or FaceTime because the border has been closed.

There has been so much sorrow, it feels like too much to deal with. No one can come to help. My anxiety is stacking. I fear another loss coming. I asked Aaron if he can give me some guidance on how to handle this situation. His answer was immediate and wise. He said, "Mom, the universe is your guide, flow with it." This advice is exactly what I needed to hear to adjust my thinking. My anxiety lowered. Thank you, Aaron.

Sunday November 29, 2020

My father passed this morning. His nurse called to tell me that his passing was peaceful. In a way, it helped me to hear that. I still feel traumatized from losing Aaron. I think I'm suffering from PTSD.

I lost my mother only four months before Aaron. I witnessed her death. She died from severe sepsis. It was a complication of her chemotherapy treatment for leukemia. The ICU doctor called me to come in to consent for her removal from life support. When I arrived, he and a nurse sympathetically explained the situation. I told them that I had been a critical care nurse, and I fully understood. That was my first mistake.

When they heard that, they escorted me to my mother's bedside and turned off her ventilator. I stood there holding her hand as it went cold. I was frozen in place watching her turn blue as she struggled for air. I can't believe they walked me into that. They should have known better. Too bad that I used to be a nurse. She was my mother. They should have known. I haven't been able to get the image of that scene out of my mind. I am still traumatized by it.

I asked Aaron and my mother if my father is with them. My mother said, "He's on his way here." Aaron said, "He's still hanging around his body because it just happened. He's figuring it out. His energy is flowing toward us."

Friday December 4, 2020.

Anthony and I came up to the cottage for the insulation installation. It was an all-day job. The cottage is warmer now. We figure that we'll spend a lot of time here in the winter. Especially during the winter of Covid-19 when we won't be travelling anywhere else.

Today, I got it in my head to put up a tree for Christmas and Hanukkah. We saw the right tree, a white one with white twinkle lights, in a flier ad. So, we drove the 30 minutes to Peterborough to get that tree. A white tree with blue and silver ornaments would fit the theme of both holidays. I was excited to put up our Chrismukkah tree before the kids came.

At the same time, I was feeling unsure if Aaron would like it. While putting up the tree, I began to have second thoughts. I went back and forth in my mind while hanging the ornaments, even though I took great care to display them in an eye-pleasing way. Blue jays with feathers, silver sparkling butterflies, and blue with silver balls of varying sizes were carefully placed in balance around the tree.

When I took a step back to look at my work, I thought, *"It looks okay."* Just okay. I told Anthony that the tree looked beautiful and generic at the same time. It needed something personal.

Sunday December 6, 2020.

I went into town to see if I could find a couple of sentimental ornaments for the tree. There was a large display of Christmas items that occupied one whole corner of a store. There were so many ornaments on display, it was dizzying to look through them all for the right one.

I spotted a Bambi and Mother ornament. "Bambi" was Aaron's favourite movie when he was a year old. I played that VHS for him over and over. When the movie was finished, Aaron would say, "Again!" Of course, I would put it on again. Seeing the ornament made me cry, but I bought it anyway. I just couldn't walk away from that

158

memory. I chose a couple more ornaments that reflected some memories of the kids when they were young.

I headed for the cashier. Just before the counter, there were two shelves of ornaments separate from the others. A sign above them said, "2019 Ornaments $5 and $10 cash, Proceeds to Charity". In the very center of the first shelf was an ornament unlike all the others.

It was a Hanukkah ornament with a Menorah and a Star of David on it. At first, I thought I was seeing things. I've never seen a Hanukkah ornament. Yet, there it was on the shelf, right in my eyeline. On the box, it said, "2019". What was it doing there?

It was meant to be that I would find it. It was a sign from Aaron that he's okay with the Chrismukkah tree. The Hanukkah ornament is now hanging front and center of the tree where everyone can see it.

Hanukkah Tree
Ornament

Monday December 14, 2020.

My father's funeral was this morning. I was worried about
how it would be with only a few of us in attendance due to
Covid. I was wrong to worry. We made it quite significant.
All my kids came, including Caleb. Anthony and Candice
were there too. Jonathan played taps for my father. It was
a beautiful salute to him.

I asked Aaron about fear of death. It seemed to me that it
was the only thing my father feared. "Fear of death is part
of survival instinct, Mom. It's normal to be afraid of it.
Human existence is part of universal energy flow, so is
human survival."

Tuesday December 15, 2020.

I asked Aaron today if he could explain to me what I should be doing since I'm still alive. He said that it doesn't matter what I do, as long as it's done with kindness and love. He said that this is most important. "Mom, you don't need to wonder, or search for meaning, as long as you treat everyone and everything with love. Love is the energy of the universe. You will find love for others within yourself, and you'll find their love for you within yourself too. That goes for everyone."

I had to drive to Markham to pick up my father's things that we moved to the nursing home that he never moved in to. On the way there I turned on my Podcast App. I've been listening to podcasts a lot lately. This time, an episode of "Messages of Hope" with Suzanne Giesemann came on.[11] In it, Suzanne interviews Mabel Chan, author of "The Infinite Bond: My Son's Messages from Across the Veil"[12]. I was spell bound. Mabel's son, Leo sounded so much like Aaron, and he was giving his mother messages too. From this, I found the Facebook Group, Helping Parents Heal, where there is constant emotional and spiritual support between grieving parents.

All I could think about was that I need to get back to writing. I felt like it was a message to me. Plus, on Sunday,

---

[11] 10. "Messages of Hope", "Mabel Chan Interview with Suzanne Geisemann", November 19, 2020, Apple Podcast, https://www.suzannegiesemann.com/?s=mabel+chan
[12] "The Infinite Bond: My Son's Messages From Across the Veil", by Mabel Chan, September 29, 2020, Mabel Chan

Arlene reminded me that Aaron told her to tell me to write everything down. Arlene said that she's sure this will become a book. I told you she was psychic.

Wednesday December 16, 2020.

Tonight, I went to the Helping Parents Heal Group on Facebook for support. The first post I saw was from, none other than, Mabel Chan. I gave her post a "Like" emoji and commented that I heard her interview with Suzanne Giesemann, which I found very inspiring. I did not expect a response. But Mabel responded. She said that she believes that our sons brought us together, and she'd like to hear what I think of her book. I wrote back that I think our sons must be friends, they sound very much alike. She agreed. How is that for timing!

Thursday December 17, 2020.

I can ask Aaron anything. I can ask him for answers to the big questions that seem to have no answer, like *"Why do kids get sick?"*, and *"Why do kids die?"* Aaron's answer came right away. He said that the complicated answer is really very simple. "Many things occur together to produce a person, and they are all flowing with the universe at varying rates. Age, illness, and death are not separate from life. The elements of life exist forever, before birth and after death, and so does the consciousness of everything." His answer sounds both simple and not simple. I think he is reassuring me that our spirits are eternal.

Friday December 18, 2020.

Aaron has been sending me messages about love. He said that he knows he was loved unconditionally for sure now. He said that the human capacity to love is bound by the physical existence. "The brain limits the ability to feel love freely and universally. There can be conflict between the spirit soul and the ego. The ego protects the self in life. It can be overprotective or under protective. It can often be hard to balance. Universal love is unconditional love of self and others. That is the wisdom here. Total openness to universal love exists in my dimension."

Tuesday December 22, 2020.

I get so many of those scam phone calls that I don't answer my home phone anymore. It's disturbing to think that there are enough people fooled by fraudsters for this to grow to the level it has. Some days my phone rings constantly. Today there was a call from an area code that I haven't seen yet, 913. It stood out for that reason. Otherwise, I wouldn't have paid it any attention.

Tonight, I was watching a medium on TV who spoke about spirit encounters. She mentioned the 913 Area Code a few times. How coincidental. What were the odds of that on the same day? I wondered what it meant.

Thursday December 24, 2020.

Early this morning when I was just beginning to wake up, with my eyes still mostly closed, I saw strings of white light dancing just above my head. The strings glowed in the unlit room. They twisted and swirled. Then they began to break up into smaller pieces and form shapes and letters. There was a heart-shaped white glowing string dancing through the letters. The letters clearly spelled the words, "I LOVE YOU". I love you too Aaron.

Saturday December 26, 2020.

We had a white Christmas yesterday. The falling snow gives you a peaceful feeling. This morning is so quiet. Inside where it's warm, I took a look at my security camera screen to see if our street had been ploughed. To my amazement, I saw letters in the snow, some in English and some in Hebrew.

They appeared to spell "AHAVAמאד" (Ahava may-ohd). The whole two words were written from right to left as in Hebrew, but the first word, AHAVA was written in the English alphabet backwards, and the second word was written in the Hebrew aleph-bet correctly. There's even an exclamation mark at the beginning! The two Hebrew words mean, "Love Very Much" in English.

I am sure Aaron wrote me this message, and that he made sure that I saw it.

Words In The Snow

Friday January 1, 2021.

We quietly entered our second New Year without Aaron. We're at the cottage with Caleb. He's providing me with a lot of distraction from my grief. Having a grandchild is fun work. The day is full of indoor and outdoor activities. It warms my heart to spend time with him. It's good for both him and I. He has been needing this time spent out in nature for a long time after being cooped up from the Covid-19 lockdowns.

Nature is soothing and nurturing. That's why we call it "Mother". Any time that I spend outdoors I feel calm and comforted. Like Aaron says, we enter an exchange of compatible energy when we immerse ourselves in nature. We feel closer to the source of our creation.

Covid-19 is still around. I have to admit, I haven't minded the social restrictions since I'm grieving. Plus, the Covid vogue matches my grief wear, so no one can tell the difference. I can go for a walk in my pajamas. This is not to say that the pandemic is working for me, it's not.

When I do meet with people it's by videoconference and usually on "Zoom". The app exploded on to the scene last year as a platform for video-teleconferencing. It has become the new normal for business to carry on. People can work from home. Kids can do their school lessons online. The world is connected even though we're isolated. We depend on our connections.

The news is reporting an expected increase in cases after the holidays due to social gatherings. I'm hoping people will use some uncommon common sense and defer their celebrations to next year. But I won't hold my breath. There are people still calling this a hoax.

The Covid-19 pandemic has brought out the best and the worst in people. "Covidiots". There's a new word for Webster. It's becoming as overused as "zeitgeist", and "de rigeur". Funny how you can put together a sentence using all three of those words that would fit the current times.

People are so divided. Both sides think the other side are the "Covidiots". Some of the same people are both anti-maskers and anti-lockdowners. They miss the obvious self-contradiction. They ignore the science.

What will it take for people to wake up? We are up against much bigger forces than each other. Universal forces are unseen and greater than we know. Hasn't this pandemic taught us that?

Some people are already "woke". On the front lines of this pandemic are our heroes. Doctors, nurses, medical staff, personal care workers, paramedics, firefighters, police, our leaders, the list is long. They risk their lives every day to care for others. They care unselfishly and unconditionally. They never ask for awards or praise, but they are the most deserving.

The timing of Aaron's message seems never better. Of course, this makes it sound like it was a good time for him to pass. I don't want to connect those dots. I just want to channel his voice and get his message out.

Saturday January 2, 2021.

It's early morning and I can hear the thunders and moans coming from the frozen lake. Sometimes, it's so joltingly loud. Other times it sounds like distant whale calls. There are no whales in this lake. It's the sound of the water flowing beneath the ice.

People go for walks on the lake ice. It hasn't been cold enough yet for me to feel safe on it. But I see some cross-country skiers, snow shoers, and the occasional snowmobiler out there having fun. There's even an ice fishing hut near the island. You won't catch me out there, no pun intended.

We had a beautiful snow fall yesterday. Today, it's bright and sunny. The sun is sparkling on the blanket of fresh snow. We're going for a hike and some sledding at a great nearby trail.

Grief caught me by surprise when we arrived. Memories of pulling Aaron in a sled when he was Caleb's age came pouring in. I stopped in my tracks on the trail as the tears began to flow. This was not a good time for a grief attack, but there seems to be no control over when they come.

I asked Aaron to please give me an obvious sign that I can't miss. The scenery was spectacularly distracting, and I took out my camera to capture some footage of the winter wonderland.

While my video was running, I caught an image of Aaron's sign. I call it, "Snow Falling Like Angel Dust".

Snow Falling Like Angel Dust

Monday January 4, 2021.

Horoscopes. They're fun to read once in a while, but that's as far as it goes. Astrology is mysterious and complicated. There's no science to support its veracity. I haven't read my horoscope since Aaron passed. I don't want to know.

I used to think of astrology as hocus pocus. I'm not so sure it is anymore. Based on Aaron's messages, we are made of the same stuff as the celestial bodies. We are eternally connected to everything throughout space and time. That's astrology essentially, isn't it?

I've been having recent thoughts about when to end this book. Our story will never be over. I don't want this journal to ever end. But it feels like now is the right time to get Aaron's message out. I can sense Aaron pushing me to get it finished so people can read it. "Get it done, Mom." Maybe, "Aaron's Energy" will give someone hope and help to improve their experience with loss and grief.

This morning I got a spam email with my horoscope. What the heck, I opened it. Aaron made sure I did. It said, "It's time to get back out there Leo...in 2021...find a publisher for that amazing manuscript."

> It's time to get back out there, Leo. The world needs your genius in 2021, and the stars are encouraging you to make a big statement this year. Launch that project, commit to your art or find a publisher for that amazing manuscript. Whatever you've been working on behind the scenes this past year, it's time for a big reveal.

My Horoscope

Thursday February 4, 2021.

Today on a hike I heard a lot from Aaron. It was a gorgeous and sunny day. As soon as I realized that I was enjoying the trail and the exercise, I felt guilty. Aaron told me, "Mom, I'm with you and enjoying the hike too. I can even feel the fitness of it." I was instantly comforted and carried on. I asked Aaron if my mother was there with us too. He said, "Yes Mom. Mimi is here and Pipi is too." I asked him if they're also enjoying our walk at their ages being elderly when they passed. Aaron said, "Mimi is 37, and Pipi is 40, and they are happy. Here, you can be in any time that feels good. You're their child now where they are." But my father was in the Vietnam war when he was forty years old. Why would he be happy then? "There are no wars here, Mom. Here is where everything gets fixed."

I'm listening Aaron. We're in this together all the way.

I love you forever.

"Mom, everyone is a significant part of the whole eternal story. There is not, nor has there ever been, one person, animal, insect, plant, molecule, or atom that has not been an essential part of our universe. Every bit of energy that makes up everything is timeless, loving, creating, and recreating. Not one manifestation is of more value than another. Not one part can be taken away. Imagine a car that is missing an axle clip. The salesman tells you that it isn't an important part. Would you buy the car? Would you drive it? Imagine an airplane missing a wing flap screw that the pilot tells you isn't necessary. Suddenly, you're thinking that this particular screw is the most important part of the plane. Everyone matters. Never underestimate or overestimate yourself. Everyone and everything are equally invaluable. Unite, cooperate, and feel your energy flow in balance with the energy of the universe. Our love is forever. We are one."

This might be the end of the book, but it's not the end of the story.

My mission is accomplished. Now, on to Aaron's.

One Soul

The world sees your reflection in my mirror.

Your love is in my eyes.

Your wisdom is heard in my voice.

Your warmth is felt in my embrace.

Your pride is my posture.

Your presence is palpated in my heart.

The world sees your value in my grief.

We are part of each other.

Forever together through time and space.

Souls conjoined.

Camille Dan 2020

Update

Wednesday, April 14, 2021

This story truly never ends. So much has happened since I wrote the first edition of "Aaron's Energy". I have read more books, and I have met so many amazing people who I might never have. Of course, I would give anything to have Aaron physically here with me. But reality is what it is, and I have to keep putting one foot in front of the other in this journey.

Aaron still sends me amazing signs and messages, perfectly timed so I can connect the dots for meaning. He tells me that we work together from both sides across the veil.

Last evening as I looked out over the peaceful lake at our cottage, I asked Aaron for a sign. A bright light appeared in the water. When I looked to the sky, a radiant angel hovered among the clouds. I asked Aaron if he was the angel. He said, "We are the angel, Mom."

Then, overlapping rings of ripple effects began to appear in the lake water, one by one, expanding across each other. I knew Aaron's message as soon as I saw it. We are energy, light, and waves, connecting, intersecting, sharing, and crossing paths as we flow across the universe.

Angel of Light Over the Lake

Acknowledgements

My deepest gratitude and appreciation for the guidance, love, generosity, and support that went into the writing of this book, to the following goes:

Foremost to my beloved son, Aaron, of blessed memory, the primary author of this book.

To my talented son, and devoted brother of Aaron, Jonathan, who provided the cover art.

To my wonderful, loving children, and Aaron's siblings, Zachary, Jonathan, and Shelby for honouring Aaron, and for being integral to this whole journey.

To my forever friend, Arlene, without whose intervention, knowledge, clairvoyance, and encouragement this book would not have been written.

To my dearest Anthony who remained by my side, holding me up through the most tragic and traumatic loss of my life, whose compassionate understanding has provided me the strength to carry on, and who patiently listened to me read what I wrote.

To my enlightened father-in-law, Leslie, who provided me resources and opportunities for spiritual connection with Aaron.

To my cherished friend, Cynthia, who brought me comfort and opportunities for further spiritual connections.

To my enchanted friend, Lorraine, who gave me advice and direction to follow possibilities.

To my phenomenal friend, Catherine, who shared her deepest grief with mine, and who provided me comfort and expert writing advice.

To my invincible friend, Karin, whose heart, and door are always open to me and to all in need of shelter no matter who they are or how many legs they walk on.

To my thoughtful friend, Laura, who offered me balanced insight and empathy.

To Rabbi Elie and Mordechai, whose concern and guidance for my family and I through our worst tragedy were deeds of utmost kindness.

To Helping Parents Heal, www.helpingparentsheal.org

To every one of my family and friends on both sides of the veil, too many to name, who have faith in me, and push me to keep going, who entrusted their stories to me, and who shared my belief that "Aaron's Energy" would be a light unto the world.

Proceeds from the sales of this book will go towards mental health and addiction care and research, and bereavement services, internationally. Links to purchase at www.aaronsenergy.com

References and Recommended Reading

1. "Resilient Grieving: Finding Strength and Embracing Life After a Loss That Changes Everything" by Lucy Hone, Foreword by Karen Reivich, 2017, The Experiment LLC, NY, NY
2. "Many Lives, Many Masters: The True Story of a Psychiatrist, His Young Patient, and Past-Life Therapy" by Brian L. Weiss M.D. (Author, Narrator), 1988, Simon & Schuster, NY
3. "It's OK That You're Not OK: Meeting Grief and Loss in a Culture That Doesn't Understand" by Megan Devine, Foreword by Mark Nepo, 2017, Sounds True, Boulder Colorado
4. "Breathe Cry Breathe: From Sorrow to Strength in the Aftermath of Sudden, Tragic Loss" by Catherine Gourdier, May 11, 2021, HarperCollinsCanada
5. "Refuge In Grief, Megan Devine, https://refugeingrief.com/
6. "How to Change Our Self-Limiting Programs" by Chip Richards, November 13, 2015, upliftconnect.com, Dr. Bruce Lipton
7. "Sanctuary in Five Dimensions" by Alexander Poltorak, Quantum Torah, Disentangling The Bible, July 27, 2018, https://www.quantumtorah.com/sanctuary-in-five-dimensions
8. "Beyond Weird: Why Everything You Thought You Knew about Quantum Physics Is Different", by Philip Ball, October 18, 2018 University of Chicago Press
9. Limitless Manifestations Keys", Ziad Masri, Facebook
10. "Reality Unveiled: The Hidden Keys of Existence That Will Transform Your Life (and The World)", by Ziad Masri, 2017, Awakened Media LLP

11. "Messages of Hope", "Mabel Chan Interview with Suzanne Giesemann", November 19, 2020, Unity Online Radio, Apple Podcast, https://www.suzannegiesemann.com/?s=mabel+chan

12. "The Infinite Bond: My Son's Messages From Across the Veil", by Mabel Chan, September 29, 2020, Mabel Chan

13. "General Relativity & Curved Spacetime Explained!", "The Geometry of Causality", "Is Gravity an Illusion?" Space Time, PBS Digital Studios

14. "Proof of Heaven: A Neurosurgeon's Journey into the Afterlife", by Eben Alexander, M.D., October 23, 2012, Simon&Schuster

15. "The Light Between Us: Stories From Heaven. Lessons for the Living", by Laura Lynne Jackson, July 5, 2016, The Dial Press

16. "Life After Life", by Raymond A. Moody, Junior, M.D., September 8, 2015, HarperOne

17. "The Unspeakable Loss: How do you live after a child dies?", by Nisha Zenoff, PhD, November 7, 2017, Da Capo Lifelong Books

18. "Same Soul, Many Bodies: Discover the Healing Power of Future Lives Through Progression Therapy", by Brian L. Weiss M.D., November 3, 2004, Free Press

19. "Messages of Hope: The Metaphysical Memoir of a Most Unexpected Medium", by Suzanne Giesemann, March 24, 2012, Lightning Source Inc.

20. "We Don't Die: A Skeptic's Discovery of Life After Death", by Sandra Champlain, Forward by Bernie Siegel, Jan. 1, 2013, Morgan James Publishing

21. "The Afterlife of Billy Fingers: How My Bad-Boy Brother Proved to Me There's Life After Death",

by Annie Kagan, Forward by Raymond Moody,
March 1, 2013, Hampton Roads Publishing

22. "One Year After: From Grief to Hope", by Elly
    Sheykhet, May 9, 2020, Alina's Light Publishing
23. "Ally's Hope: My Christmas Angel", by Margaret
    Petrozzo, May 12,2021, Independently Published
24. "The 21 Day Doorway Across The Veil", by Mary
    Bertun, Edited by Tava Wilson, April 26, 2020, Faith
    In Angels

Printed in Great Britain
by Amazon

78039596R10108